Quilt Block Bonanza

50 Paper-Pieced Designs

NANCY MAHONEY

Credits

President • *Nancy J. Martin*
CEO • *Daniel J. Martin*
VP and General Manager • *Tom Wierzbicki*
Publisher • *Jane Hamada*
Editorial Director • *Mary V. Green*
Managing Editor • *Tina Cook*
Technical Editor • *Darra Williamson*
Copy Editor • *Liz McGehee*
Design Director • *Stan Green*
Illustrator • *Laurel Strand*
Text Designer • *Trina Craig*
Cover Designer • *Stan Green*

That Patchwork Place® is an imprint of
Martingale & Company®.

Quilt Block Bonanza: 50 Paper-Pieced Designs
© 2005 by Nancy Mahoney

Martingale & Company
20205 144th Avenue NE
Woodinville, WA 98072-8478 USA
www.martingale-pub.com

Printed in China
10 09 08 07 06 05   8 7 6 5 4 3 2 1

Mission Statement

Dedicated to providing quality products and service to inspire creativity.

Library of Congress Cataloging-in-Publication Data
Mahoney, Nancy.
    Quilt block bonanza : 50 paper-pieced designs / Nancy Mahoney.
        p.   cm.
    ISBN 1-56477-612-3
1. Patchwork—Patterns.   2. Quilting.   3. Patchwork quilts.
I. Title.
    TT835.M27154985 2005
    746.46'041—dc22
                                                    2005008700

Acknowledgments

A special thank-you to all the wonderful people at Martingale & Company, especially Mary Green, Karen Soltys, Terry Martin, and Donna Lever, whose continued support and friendship made this book a reality. I also appreciate the expertise of my technical editor, Darra Williamson, and my copy editor, Liz McGehee, who made the process almost painless.

Above all, I want to thank Tom Reichert for his support and encouragement and for cheerfully enduring many evenings and weekends when I was totally preoccupied with sewing and writing.

Contents

Introduction

When I began quilting, my introduction to the wonderful world of traditional blocks was the *It's Okay If You Sit on My Quilt Book* by Mary Ellen Hopkins (Yours Truly Publications from Dale Burdett, 1982). I spent many enjoyable hours studying the blocks and sketching them on graph paper. Since then, my personal library of quilt-block reference books has grown and continues to be a source of inspiration for my quilts.

The seed for this book was planted when I was working on my first book, *Rich Traditions: Scrap Quilts to Paper Piece* (Martingale & Company, 2002). I wanted to create a collection of traditional blocks that could be pieced using paper foundation techniques. Paper foundation piecing is often described as "sewing by number" and is a great method for creating accurate patchwork blocks, especially for beginners. It's amazing to me how the desire to use this easy technique becomes the inspiration for many exciting and creative quilts.

I selected a 5" block for the patterns in this book. The size is easy to handle, and paper-piecing techniques eliminate the need to deal with measurements that fall between the ⅛" marking on most rotary rulers.

Each block pattern includes a quilt diagram that illustrates how the block will look in a quilt. In "Planning Your Quilt" (page 8), you'll find additional ideas for setting the blocks and discover that the blocks are only the beginning.

Block Basics

The following pages provide valuable information about paper-foundation-piecing techniques as well as tips for planning your quilt and calculating yardages. Instructions for finishing your quilt begin on page 10.

Using the Block Patterns

The block patterns appear in alphabetical order. Keep in mind that many traditional blocks have been given different names in different areas of the country. A block you are familiar with may be listed by another name.

A cutting chart is provided for each block pattern. Many of the patterns produce a single block. Occasionally, it is a more efficient use of fabric to cut the pieces for two or four blocks at a time. Be sure to check each pattern to see how many blocks the instructions yield. If you are using fabrics similar to those shown, simply match your color choices to those in the diagram and chart. If you have chosen a different color combination, check the size to cut for the appropriate shapes in the block and cut the pieces accordingly.

The pattern pages include full-size paper foundations for each block pattern. Because you will be sewing from the reverse side of the paper foundation, the patterns are shown as the reverse of the finished block. If you desire a specific color placement, use colored pencils to color the areas as a reminder.

Paper Foundation Piecing

Paper foundation piecing is a method of block or unit construction in which strips or cut pieces of fabric are sewn in numerical order to a paper foundation. The paper stabilizes the fabric so you don't need to be too concerned about the fabric grain, except for those pieces that fall on the outside edges of the block. Since I prefer to remove the paper before sewing the blocks together, I try to cut the outside pieces on the straight grain of the fabric.

Copying the Paper Foundations

You will need one paper foundation pattern for each block. Most copy stores will remove the binding of this book and three-hole punch it or add a spiral binding for a nominal fee. This makes it easier to copy the blocks.

Be sure to make all copies for your project on the same copy machine. Make a single copy first to ensure the shapes are not distorted before making all the copies.

For foundation piecing, you will want paper that holds up while sewing and is easy to remove afterward. Use lightweight paper or paper made specifically for foundation piecing, such as *Papers for Foundation Piecing* available from Martingale & Company. The paper doesn't need to be translucent. The light from your sewing machine is sufficient for you to see through the unmarked side to the marked pattern on the other side.

After photocopying the block pattern, trim the paper foundation ¼" from the outer (cutting) line. This makes the paper foundation easier to maneuver under the presser foot. Also, if the fabric pieces extend beyond the paper foundation, you know the pieces are large enough to allow for the seam allowance around the outer edges of the block.

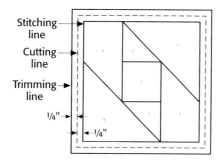

Stitching line
Cutting line
Trimming line
¼"
¼"

Selecting Fabrics

Directions for each block include a cutting chart that lists the colors of fabric for the block as shown. You'll also find a small outline drawing of four blocks positioned as they appear in the sample quilt. (In some cases, a tip suggests making blocks in different color combinations so you can duplicate the quilt shown.) You can make copies of the drawing to experiment with color placement. Changing the colors within a block can create a very different quilt. Compare the arrangement of Target blocks below to the layout on page 104. Notice how simply changing the colors in the blocks can create a totally different look.

You can also cut the outline drawing apart to experiment with the arrangement of the individual blocks in your quilt. Study the line drawings of the Next-Door Neighbor block below. The first yields the quilt shown on page 68. In the second layout, the block has been rotated 90° to create an entirely different look.

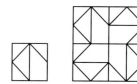

This layout is shown on page 68.

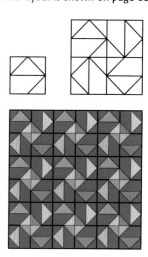

This is the same block rotated 90°.

Cutting the Pieces

The cutting chart for each block indicates how many pieces to cut, what size to cut them, and where each piece is used. When cut as directed, each piece is large enough to cover the intended area on the paper foundation plus all seam allowances. Four symbols are used throughout the book.

  ☐ = Square(s)

  ◺ = Square(s) cut once diagonally to make half-square triangles

  ⊠ = Square(s) cut twice diagonally to make quarter-square triangles

  ▭ = Rectangle(s)

If you are unfamiliar with rotary cutting, refer to Candace Eisner Strick's *The Quilter's Quick Reference Guide* (Martingale & Company, 2004) for more detailed rotary-cutting instructions.

ORGANIZING MULTIPLE SHAPES

For blocks with many pieces and similar shapes, label the stacks of cut fabrics with small stick-on notes. This will keep the pieces organized and save you time as you sew.

Sewing the Blocks

Once you have selected your block, made copies of the foundation, cut your fabric pieces, and—if needed—labeled the stacks, you are ready to sew. We'll use the Attic Window block (page 12) as our example.

1. Prepare your sewing machine with a size 90/14 needle and an open-toe presser foot, and adjust your stitch length to 14 to 16 stitches per inch. The larger needle and shorter stitch length will allow you to remove the paper easily. Don't make the stitches *too* short, however, as this will make removing stitches difficult if you sew a piece incorrectly.

2. Turn the foundation, blank (unmarked) side up. Position the fabric for piece 1, right side up, to cover area 1, plus an ample seam allowance. Using the light from your sewing machine or another light source, look through the fabric and paper to make sure area 1 is completely covered. Turn the paper and fabric over, being careful not to move the fabric, and pin the fabric in place through the marked side of the paper.

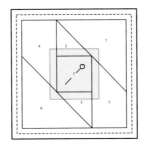

3. Once again, turn the foundation over to the unmarked side. Look through the paper and place a cut piece of fabric for piece 2, right side up, over area 2. When piece 2 is properly positioned, flip it on top of piece 1, right sides together.

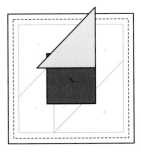

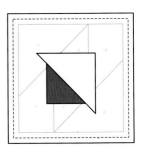

4. Hold the layers in place, turn the foundation over, and carefully position the unit under the presser foot, paper side up. Sew on the line between areas 1 and 2, starting ¼" before the line and extending ¼" beyond it.

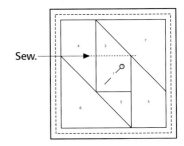

5. Remove the pin and open piece 2. Hold the block up to a light source and look through

the fabric to be sure that the edges of piece 2 extend beyond the seam lines for area 2 on the foundation.

6. Refold the fabrics and then fold the paper back to reveal the seam allowance. Place a ruler along the edge of the paper and trim the seam allowance to ¼".

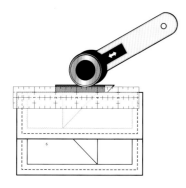

7. Open piece 2 and press the seam with a dry iron. Do not use steam. You may need to cover your ironing surface with scrap fabric to protect

the surface from any excess ink from the photocopies.

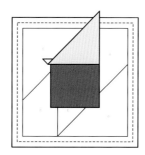

8. Trim any excess fabric if necessary.

9. Repeat steps 3–8 to add piece 3.

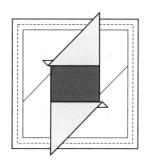

10. Continue adding the pieces in numerical order until all the pieces have been sewn to the paper foundation.

11. Turn the block paper side up. Align the ¼" line on your rotary ruler with the outside sewing line on the paper foundation. Trim the foundation and fabrics ¼" from the sewing line on all sides.

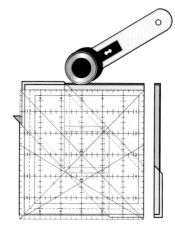

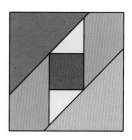

12. Remove the paper before sewing the units and blocks together.

HANDLING ODD SHAPES

When making a block with odd-shaped pieces—for example, the Morning Star block on page 56—I make an extra photocopy of the block. Next, using a rotary cutter, I cut out the odd-shaped piece on what would be the stitching line. Then I use the paper template to rough cut the odd-shaped piece from the wrong side of the fabric, making sure to include at least a ¼" seam allowance on all sides of the template.

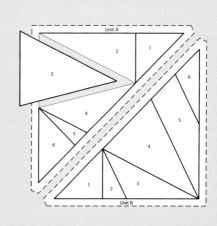

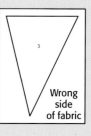

Planning Your Quilt

Whether you like to plan your quilt before making the blocks or prefer to construct the blocks before deciding on how to set them together, there are numerous setting options to consider. Each block pattern includes one example of how the block will look when set in a quilt. Most of the diagrams show the blocks in a side-by-side setting with a simple border. Many of the blocks create a secondary design when set this way, but you may also want to experiment with sashing to separate the blocks. Notice the differences in the examples below.

The Palm blocks.
Original placement

The Palm blocks
with sashing

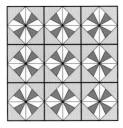

Plain Sailing blocks.
Original placement

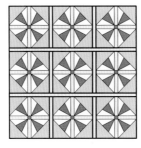

Plain Sailing blocks
with sashing

For another option, try combining two different 5" blocks and rotating them to find a pleasing arrangement. Some blocks work better together than others, so you'll want to use the outline drawings to play with the different possibilities.

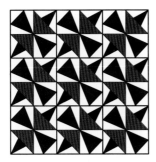

Sugar Cone blocks
and Plain Sailing blocks

Consider placing four blocks side by side to create a larger 10" block. Then separate the 10" blocks with sashing as shown below. Or make 10" blocks from two different 5" blocks, and combine the two 10" blocks to create a unique quilt design.

Eight-Pointed Star
10" block

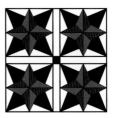

Eight-Pointed Star blocks
with sashing

Sugar Cone   Plain Sailing
10" block   10" block

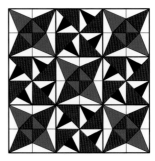

Sugar Cone blocks and
Plain Sailing blocks combined

Experiment with different arrangements: try a side-by-side setting with every other block rotated, turn the blocks on point, add plain (unpieced) alternate blocks, or create a strippy setting by arranging the blocks in horizontal or vertical rows separated with plain or pieced bars. You'll find lots of fun ideas in *Sensational Settings: Over 80 Ways to Arrange Your Quilt Blocks, Revised Edition,* by Joan Hanson (Martingale & Company, 2004).

Making Multiple Blocks

When you are using the blocks to make a quilt, you will want to avoid cutting out one block at a time, and cut all identical pieces at the same time.

Begin by checking to see how many blocks the cutting instructions yield. If the instructions yield one block, simply multiply the number of pieces in the cutting instructions by the number of blocks you wish to make. Let's use the Eight-Pointed Star (page 28) as an example. To make the quilt shown in the quilt diagram, you need 48 blocks. Multiply the numbers in the cutting instructions by 48 to cut 48 dark red, 96 white, 48 blue, 48 navy, and 48 red pieces.

For cutting instructions that yield 2 blocks, divide the desired number of blocks by 2, and multiply the number of pieces by this number. For example, if you wish to make 48 blocks, and the instructions yield 2 blocks, multiply the number of pieces by 24 because 48 ÷ 2 = 24. To make 48 blocks from a pattern that yields 4 blocks, multiply the numbers in the cutting instructions by 12 because 48 ÷ 4 = 12.

Calculating Yardage

When cutting multiple pieces from a single fabric, common practice is to cut selvage-to-selvage strips to the required width and then to crosscut the strips into squares, rectangles, or triangles. The first step to calculating the yardage for a quilt is to determine how many 5" blocks you need.

For example, if you are making the 36 blocks in the quilt diagram for the Missouri Windmills block (page 54), determine the number of orange rectangles by multiplying 36 (the number of blocks) by 1 (number of pieces for 1 block), which equals 36 rectangles.

Each of the orange rectangles measures 4½" x 5¾". To determine how many 5¾" pieces you can cut from a selvage-to-selvage strip, divide 42" (the width of the fabric) by 5¾" (the length of the rectangle), which equals 7.30. You can cut 7 full pieces from one 42" strip.

Divide the total number of rectangles needed (36) by the number of rectangles per strip (7). Because 36 ÷ 7 = 5.14, round up to the next whole number to get 6. That is the number of strips needed.

Finally, multiply the cut width of the strip (4½") by the number of strips needed (6). In this case, you will need 27" of fabric for these pieces because 4½" x 6 = 27".

Follow the same formula to determine the yardage for the other fabrics in the block. If you need to cut additional pieces from the same fabric, do the calculations for each piece, total the inches, and divide the sum by 36 to determine the total yardage required for that fabric. When I purchase fabric based on my calculations, I usually add 10% to the total, to allow for shrinkage and distortion.

Finishing Your Quilt

At this point you have completed all of your blocks, trimmed each block to 5½" square (including seam allowances) and have removed the paper foundation. As mentioned in "Planning Your Quilt" (page 8), there are many settings from which to choose. Some of the blocks require a particular setting for the overall design to become apparent, while other blocks offer numerous setting options. For more information on quilt settings and finishing your quilt, I again recommend *The Quilter's Quick Reference Guide.*

Borders

Most quilts have a border or borders that frame the pieced blocks. Borders can be simple strips of one or more fabrics. They can also be pieced or appliquéd and used in combination with plain strips. Borders can have overlapped corners, corner squares, or mitered corners.

Prepare border strips a few inches longer than you actually need; then trim them to the correct length once you know the dimensions of the center of your quilt top. To find the correct measurement for the border strips, always measure through the center of the quilt, not at the outside edges. This ensures that the borders are of equal length on opposite sides of the quilt and helps keep your quilt square.

Borders wider than 2" are

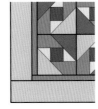 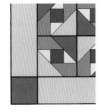

Overlapped corners   Corner squares

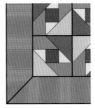

Mitered corners

usually cut on the lengthwise grain (parallel to the selvage) so they do not stretch and do not need to be pieced. For quilts smaller than 40" square, cutting strips on the crosswise grain (across the fabric from selvage to selvage) works perfectly well.

Borders less than 2" wide are usually cut from the crosswise grain and joined end to end with a diagonal seam to achieve the required length.

The simplest border to make is a border with overlapped corners. Measure the length of the quilt top through the center. Cut two border strips to this measurement, piecing as necessary. Sew them to the sides of the quilt with a ¼"-wide seam. Press the seams toward the border. Then measure the width of the quilt through the center, from side to side, including the side borders you just added. Now cut two border strips to that

measurement and sew them to the top and bottom; press.

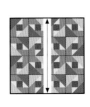 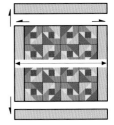

Backing and Batting

Cut a piece of fabric 4" to 6" larger than the quilt top (2" to 3" on all sides). For quilts wider than the width of your fabric, you will need to piece the backing. Unless the fabric print is best viewed from a specific direction, the seam can run horizontally or vertically; sometimes your choice can save fabric.

The batting should be large enough to allow 2" of extra batting around the edges of the quilt top.

Layering and Quilting the Quilt

Carefully press the quilt top and backing. Spread the backing, wrong side up, on a flat, clean surface. Anchor it with pins or masking tape. Center the batting over the backing, smoothing out any wrinkles. Center the pressed quilt top, right side up, on top of the batting. Smooth from the center out and along straight lines to ensure that there are no wrinkles and the blocks and borders remain straight.

For hand quilting, baste with needle and thread. Start in the center and work diagonally to each corner, basting in a grid of horizontal and vertical lines 6" to 8" apart. To finish, baste around the edges about ⅛" from the edge of the quilt top.

For machine quilting, baste with No. 2 rustproof safety pins. Place pins 4" to 6" apart; try to avoid areas where you intend to quilt.

As a general rule, unquilted areas should not exceed 4" x 4". In addition, check the packaging of the batting you are using for the recommended amount of quilting. The density of quilting should be similar throughout the entire quilt so that the quilt remains square and does not become distorted.

Binding the Quilt

When quilting is complete, trim the excess batting and backing even with the quilt top, remove all pins and basting, and square up the quilt. If you are going to attach a sleeve to the back of your quilt for hanging, attach it now, before you bind the edges.

Binding strips are generally cut 2" to 2½" wide, depending on your preference and your choice of batting. Cut enough strips to go around the perimeter of your quilt plus about 10" for seams and turning corners. Join the strips end to end with diagonal seams.

Fold the binding in half lengthwise, wrong sides together, and press. Unfold the binding at one end and turn under ¼" at a 45° angle as shown.

Fold line

Starting on the bottom edge of the quilt (not in a corner) and beginning 3" from the start of the binding, stitch the binding to the quilt with a ¼"-wide seam. Stop ¼" from the first corner and backstitch.

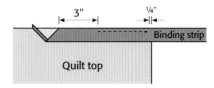
3" ¼" Binding strip
Quilt top

Remove the quilt from the sewing machine. Fold the binding away from the quilt, and then fold again as shown to create an angled pleat at the corner.

Begin with a backstitch at the fold of the binding and continue stitching along the edge of the quilt top, mitering each corner as you come to it.

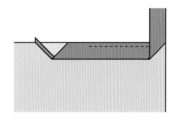

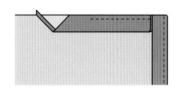

Stop 3" before the starting end of the binding and backstitch. Remove the quilt from the machine. Trim the end of the binding 1" longer than needed and tuck it inside the beginning strip. Pin in place, making sure the strip remains flat. Finish stitching the binding.

Turn the binding to the back of the quilt. Using thread that matches the binding, hand stitch the binding so the folded edge covers the row of machine stitching. At each corner, fold the binding to form a miter on the back of the quilt.

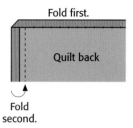
Fold first.
Quilt back
Fold second.

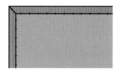

Adding a Label

A label provides important information, including the name of the quilt, the person who made it, when, and where. You may also want to include the name of the recipient if it is a gift and any other interesting or important information about the quilt. A label can be as elaborate or as simple as you desire. You can sign your name on the back of the finished quilt using a permanent marker, purchase pretty labels preprinted on fabric, or you can make your own label. You'll find lots of ideas and instruction for labels in *One-of-a-Kind Quilt Labels: Unique Ideas for a Special Finishing Touch* by Thea Nerud (Martingale & Company, 2004).

Attic Window

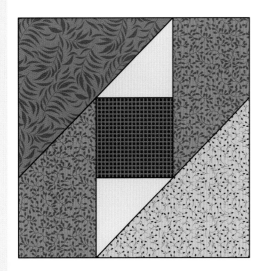

The following cutting list yields 2 blocks.

Fabric	Number of Pieces	Size to Cut	Location Number
Blue	2 □	2½" x 2½"	1
Cream	2 ◩	2¾" x 2¾"	2, 3
Purple	4 ▭	2½" x 4¼"	4, 5
Floral	1 ◩	3½" x 3½"	6
Green	1 ◩	3½" x 3½"	7

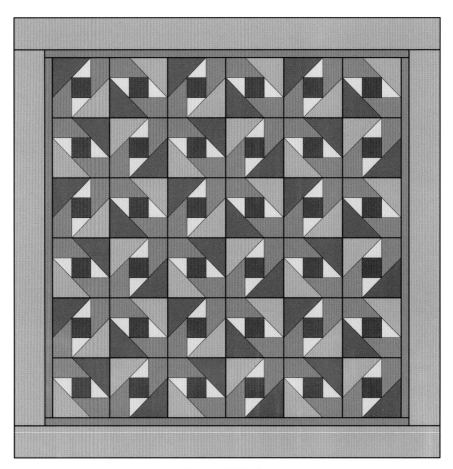

6 rows of 6 blocks

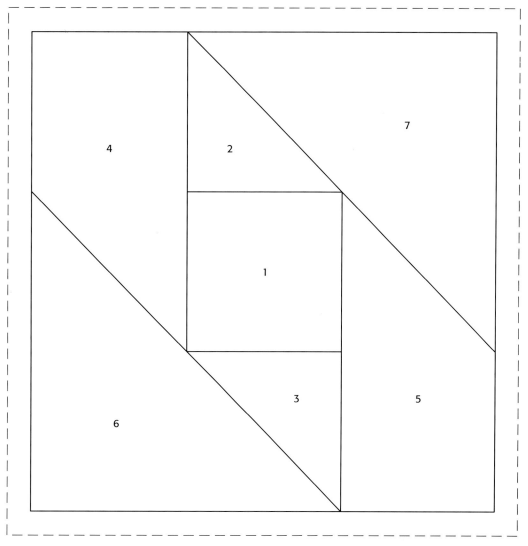

Attic Window
Foundation pattern

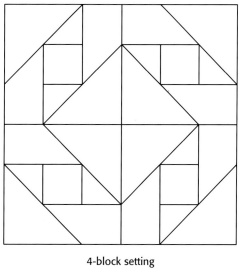

4-block setting

Bear's Paw

The following cutting list yields 1 block.

Fabric	Number of Pieces	Size to Cut	Location Number
Cream	2 ◻	2¾" x 2¾"	A1, A3, B1, B3
	1 ◻	2½" x 2½"	B5
Red	2 ◻	2¾" x 2¾"	A2, A4, B2, B4
Floral	1 ◻	4¼" x 4¼"	A5

8 rows of 6 blocks with sashing

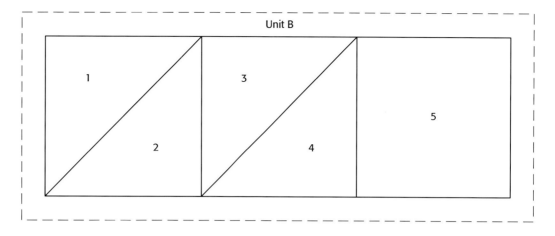

Unit B

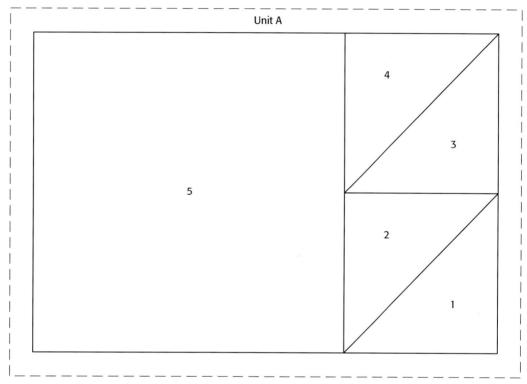

Unit A

Bear's Paw
Foundation patterns

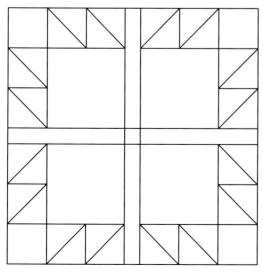

4-block setting with sashing

Beginner's Fancy

The following cutting list yields 2 blocks.

Fabric	Number of Pieces	Size to Cut	Location Number
Medium dark blue	2 ☐	2½" x 2½"	1
Cream	8 ◹	2½" x 2½"	2, 3, 4, 5, 8, 9, 10, 11
Dark blue	4 ◹	2¾" x 2¾"	6, 7, 12, 13
Light blue	1 ◹	4½" x 4½"	14
Medium light blue	1 ◹	4½" x 4½"	15

8 rows of 6 blocks

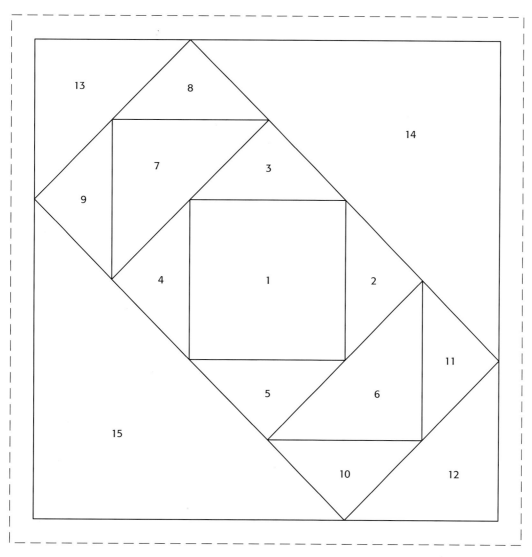

Beginner's Fancy
Foundation pattern

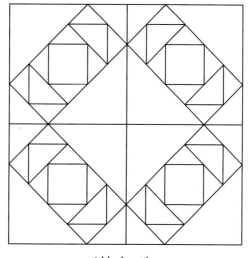

4-block setting

Cart Wheels

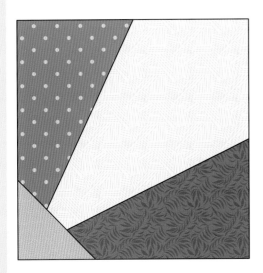

The following cutting list yields 2 blocks.

Fabric	Number of Pieces	Size to Cut	Location Number
Cream	2 ▭	4¼" x 6¾"	1
Green	2 ▭	3¾" x 5¼"	2
Rose	2 ▭	3¾" x 5¼"	3
Tan	1 ◹	2¾" x 2¾"	4

6 rows of 6 blocks

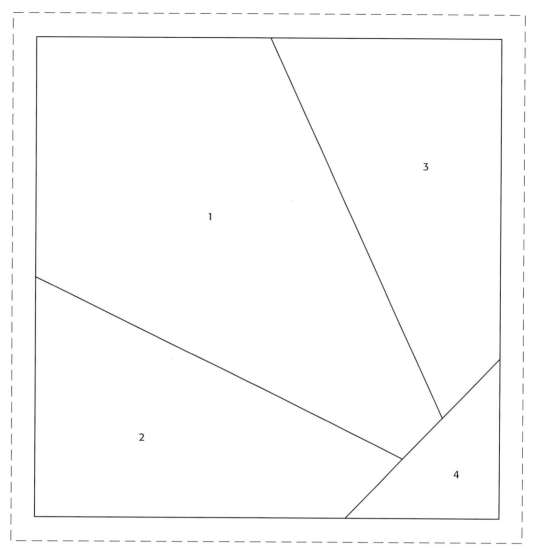

Cart Wheels
Foundation pattern

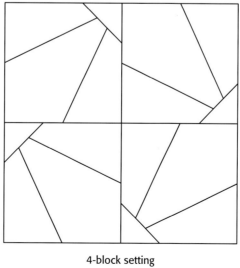

4-block setting

Cracker

The following cutting list yields 1 block.

Fabric	Number of Pieces	Size to Cut	Location Number
Gold	1 ▭	2" x 4¼"	1
	1 ◩	3¾" x 3¾"	4, 6
Dark blue	2 ▭	2" x 4¼"	2, 3
	1 ◩	3¾" x 3¾"	5, 7

6 rows of 6 blocks

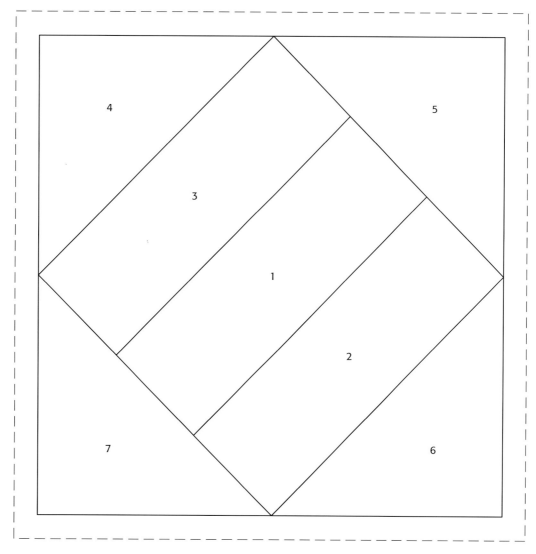

Cracker
Foundation pattern

FOR A DIFFERENT LOOK

Try switching the location of the colors in these blocks as shown in the quilt on the facing page.

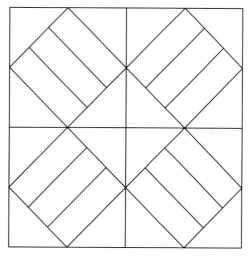

4-block setting

Crazy Pinwheels

The following cutting list yields 2 blocks.

Fabric	Number of Pieces	Size to Cut	Location Number
Green	2 ▭	2½" x 5"	1
Turquoise	2 ▭	2½" x 5"	2
Royal blue	2 ▭	3" x 5½"	3
Lavender	2 ▭	3" x 5½"	4
Dark blue	2 ▭	1¼" x 4½"	5
Red	2 ▭	1¼" x 4½"	6
Orange	1 ◺	2¾" x 2¾"	7
Yellow	1 ◺	3¾" x 3¾"	8

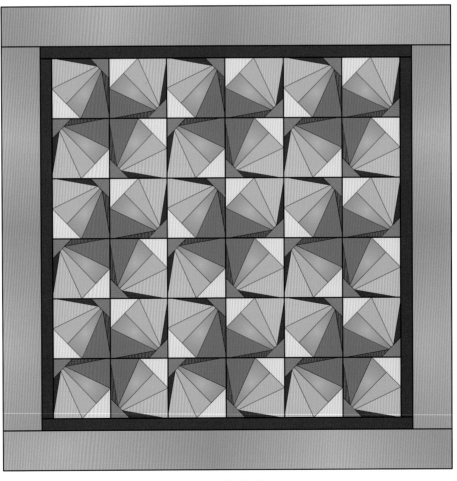

6 rows of 6 blocks

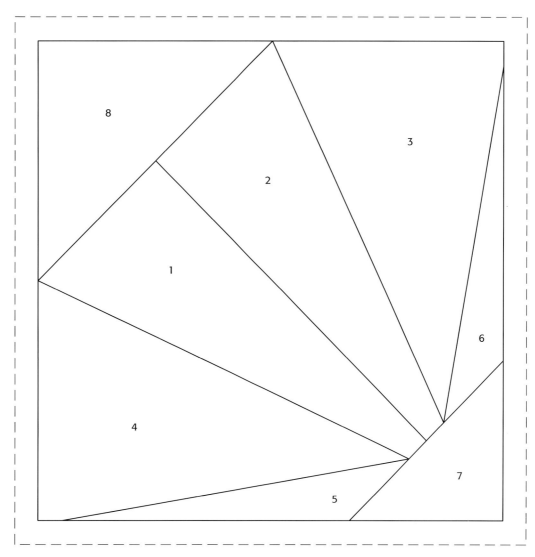

Crazy Pinwheels
Foundation pattern

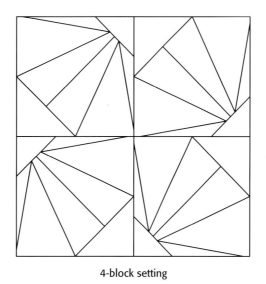

4-block setting

Double Star

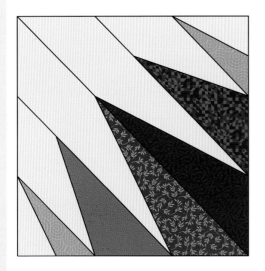

The following cutting list yields 1 block.

Fabric	Number of Pieces	Size to Cut	Location Number
Cream	2 ▭	1½" x 2¾"	A1, B1
	2 ▭	2" x 4½"	A3, B3
	2 ▭	2" x 6¾"	A5, B5
Gold	2 ▭	1½" x 3¼"	A2, B2
Dark green	1 ▭	2" x 4¼"	A4
Dark red	1 ▭	2" x 5½"	A6
Moss green	1 ▭	2" x 4¼"	B4
Red	1 ▭	2" x 5½"	B6

6 rows of 6 blocks

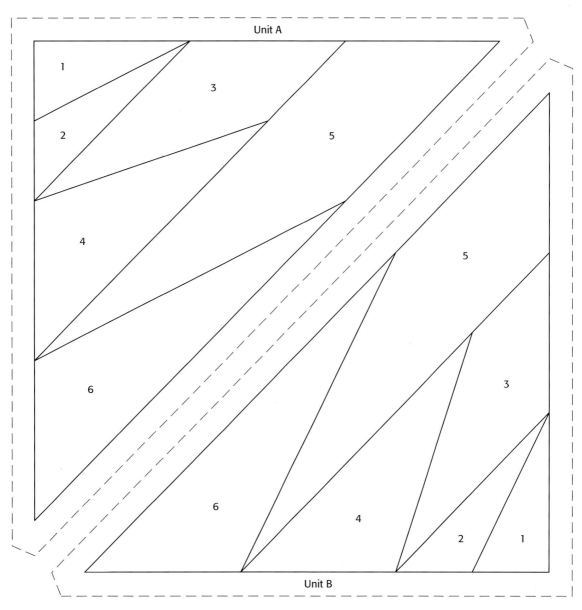

Unit A

1
3
2
5
4
5
6
3
6
4
2
1

Unit B

Double Star
Foundation patterns

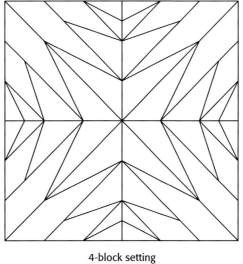

4-block setting

Dutchman's Puzzle

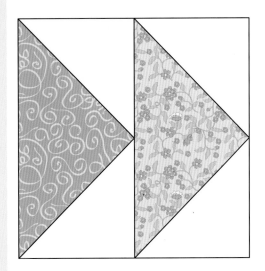

The following cutting list yields 4 blocks.

Fabric	Number of Pieces	Size to Cut	Location Number
Medium purple	1 ⊠	6½" x 6½"	1
Cream	8 ◻	3¾" x 3¾"	2, 3, 5, 6
Light purple	1 ⊠	6½" x 6½"	4

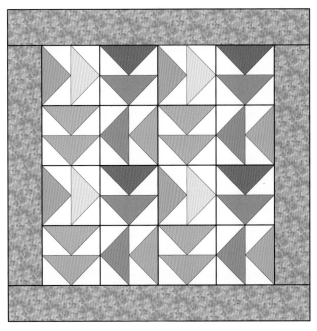

4 rows of 4 blocks

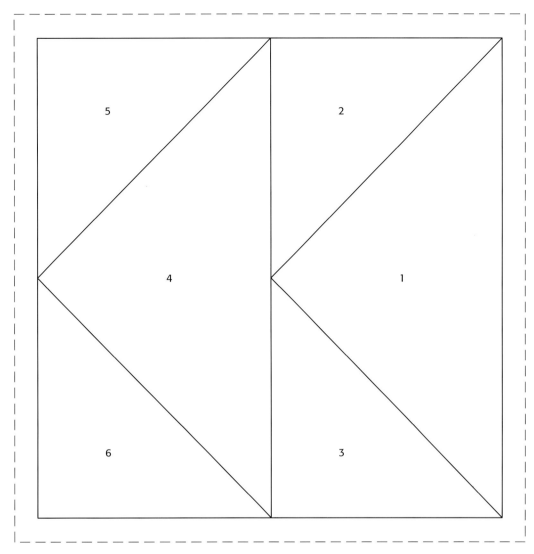

Dutchman's Puzzle
Foundation pattern

FOR A DIFFERENT LOOK

Try making these blocks in a variety of scrappy combinations as shown in the quilt on the facing page.

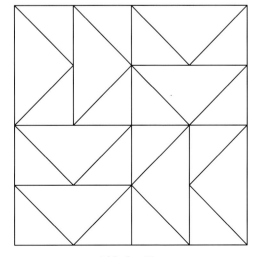

4-block setting

Eight-Pointed Star

The following cutting list yields 1 block.

Fabric	Number of Pieces	Size to Cut	Location Number
Dark red	1	2¾" x 5½"	A1
White	2	2¾" x 5¾"	A2, B1
Blue	1	2½" x 5¾"	A3
Navy	1	2¾" x 5½"	B2
Red	1	2½" x 5¾"	B3

8 rows of 6 blocks

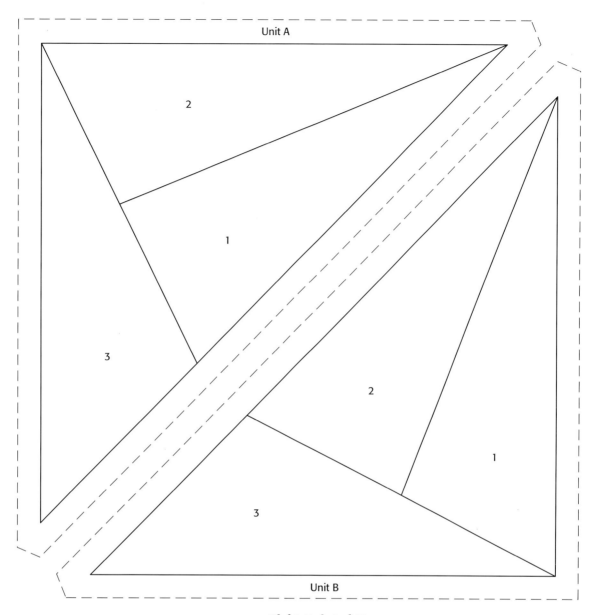

Unit A

2

1

3

2

1

3

Unit B

Eight-Pointed Star
Foundation patterns

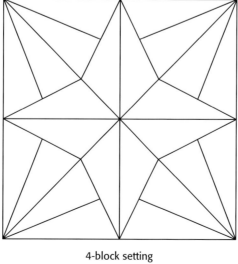

4-block setting

Flutterbye

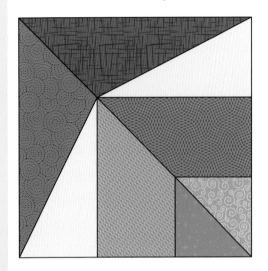

The following cutting list yields 2 blocks.

Fabric	Number of Pieces	Size to Cut	Location Number
Reddish violet	2	2½" x 5¾"	A1
Cream	4	2½" x 4½"	A2, B3
Dark blue	2	2½" x 4¼"	A3
Gold	1	2¾" x 2¾"	A4
Orange	1	2¾" x 2¾"	B1
Medium blue	2	2½" x 4¼"	B2
Violet	2	2½" x 5¾"	B4

6 rows of 6 blocks

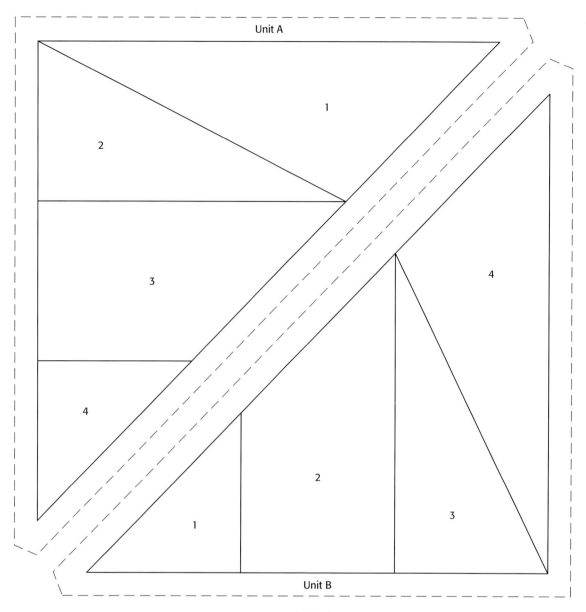

Flutterbye
Foundation patterns

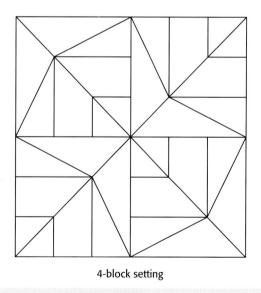

4-block setting

Flying Fish

The following cutting list yields 4 blocks.

Fabric	Number of Pieces		Size to Cut	Location Number
Navy	4	▭	2½" x 4¼"	A1
Reddish orange	4	▢	2½" x 2½"	A2
Light yellow	1	⊠	4" x 4"	A3
	2	◺	3¾" x 3¾"	A4
Gold	1	⊠	4" x 4"	B1
Royal blue	4	▭	2½" x 4¼"	B2
Light violet	1	⊠	6½" x 6½"	B3

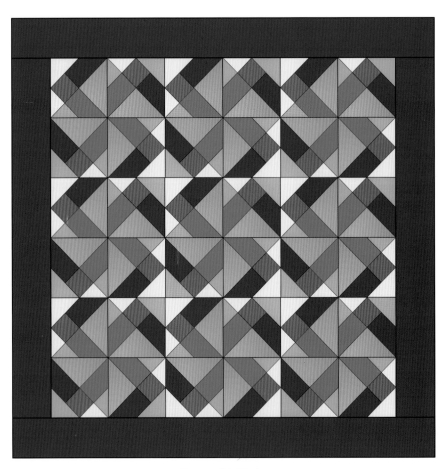

6 rows of 6 blocks

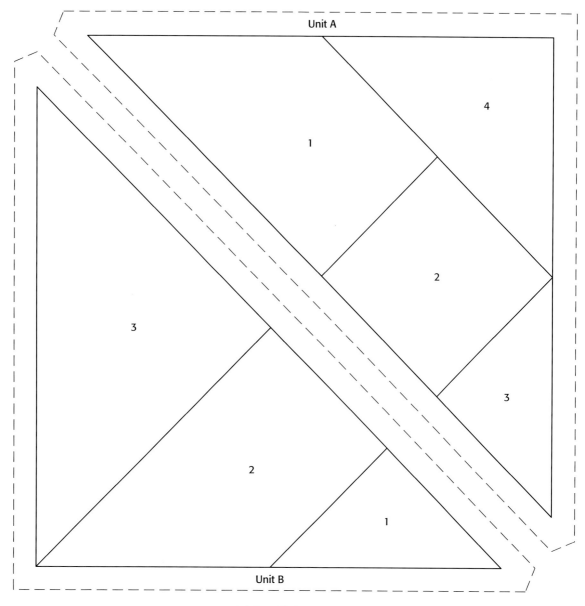

Unit A

4

1

2

3

3

2

1

Unit B

Flying Fish
Foundation patterns

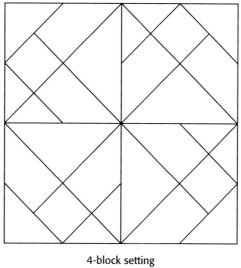

4-block setting

Flying Geese

The following cutting list yields 2 blocks.

Fabric	Number of Pieces		Size to Cut	Location Number
Cream	1	◻	2¾" x 2¾"	1
	8	◻	2¼" x 2¼"	3, 4, 6, 7, 9, 10, 12, 13
Wine	5	◻	2¾" x 2¾"	2, 5, 8, 11, 14
Red geometric	1	◻	4½" x 4½"	15
Red floral	1	◻	4½" x 4½"	16

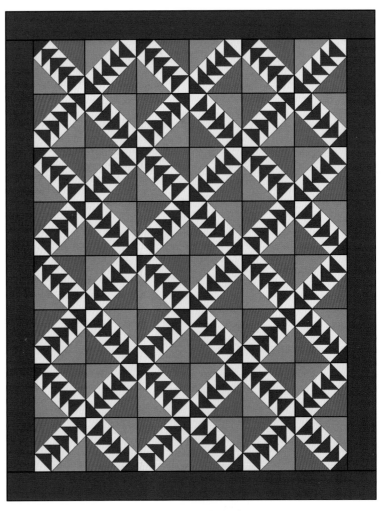

8 rows of 6 blocks

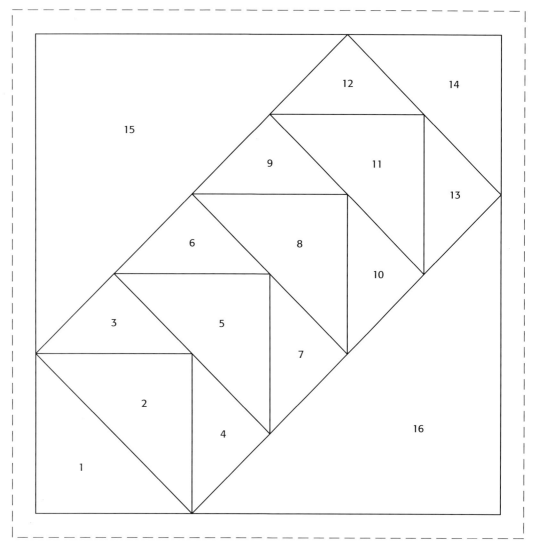

Flying Geese
Foundation pattern

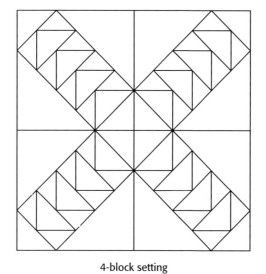

4-block setting

Flying Kites

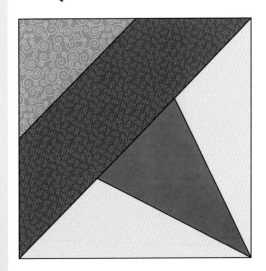

The following cutting list yields 2 blocks.

Fabric	Number of Pieces	Size to Cut	Location Number
Light yellow	4	2½" x 5¾"	1, 3
Green	2	3¼" x 4½"	2
Purple	2	2½" x 8"	4
Gold	1	3¾" x 3¾"	5

6 rows of 6 blocks

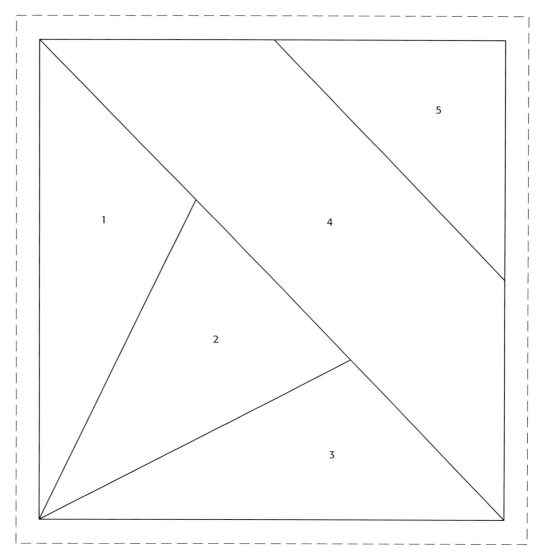

Flying Kites
Foundation pattern

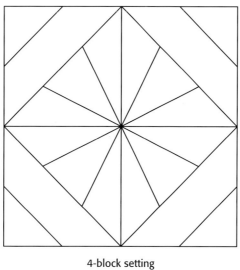

4-block setting

Flying Saucer

The following cutting list yields 1 block.

Fabric	Number of Pieces	Size to Cut	Location Number
Rust	2	2¼" x 5¾"	A1, B5
Cream	2	3½" x 4¼"	A2, B4
Black	2	2" x 4½"	A3, B3
Gold	2	1¾" x 2¾"	A4, B2
Dark brown	2	2½" x 2½"	A5, B1

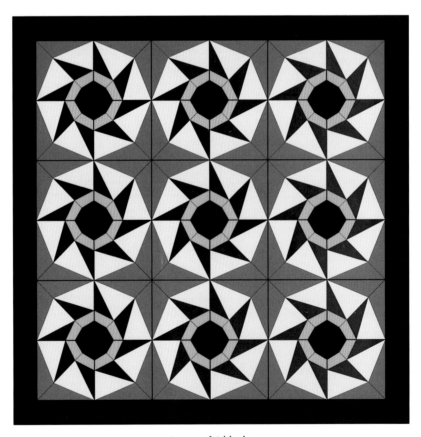

6 rows of 6 blocks

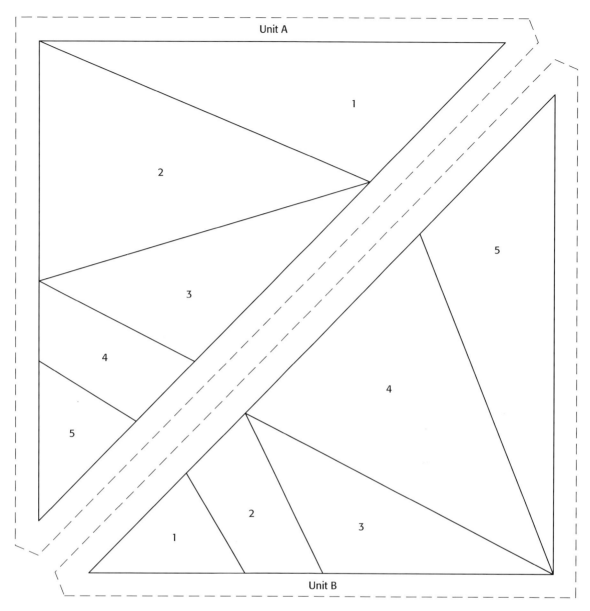

Unit A

1

2

3

4

5

5

4

Unit B

1

2

3

Flying Saucer
Foundation patterns

4-block setting

John's Pinwheel

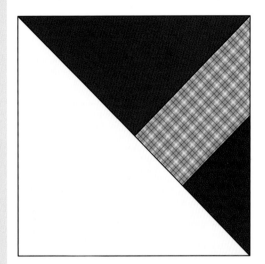

The following cutting list yields 4 blocks.

Fabric	Number of Pieces	Size to Cut	Location Number
Navy	1 ⊠	6½" x 6½"	1
Yellow geometric	4 ▭	2¼" x 4¼"	2
Red	1 ⊠	4½" x 4½"	3
Cream	2 ◺	6¼" x 6¼"	4

8 rows of 6 blocks

40

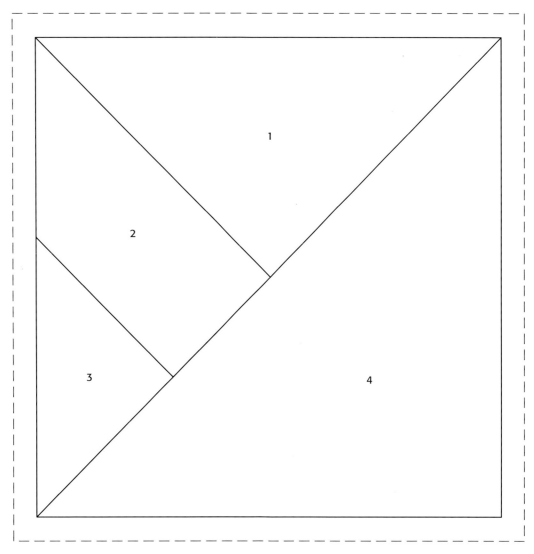

John's Pinwheel
Foundation pattern

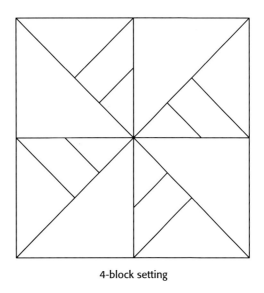

4-block setting

July Summer Sky

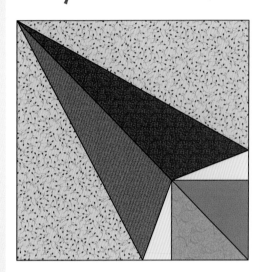

The following cutting list yields 2 blocks.

Fabric	Number of Pieces	Size to Cut	Location Number
Floral	4	3½" x 6½"	A1, B2
Dark purple	2	2¼" x 6½"	A2
Yellow	4	1½" x 2½"	A3, B3
Dark green	1	2¾" x 2¾"	A4
Medium purple	2	2¼" x 6½"	B1
Medium green	1	2¾" x 2¾"	B4

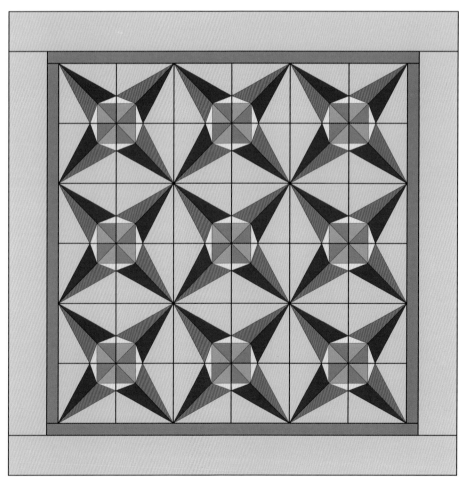

6 rows of 6 blocks

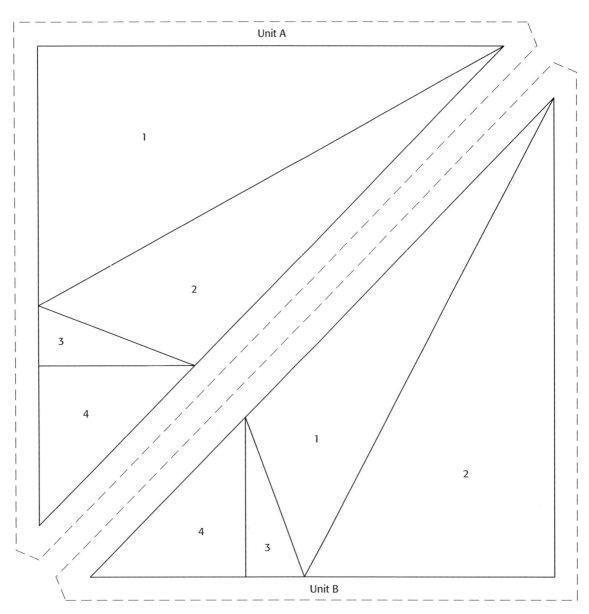

Unit A

1

2

3

4

1

2

3

4

Unit B

July Summer Sky
Foundation patterns

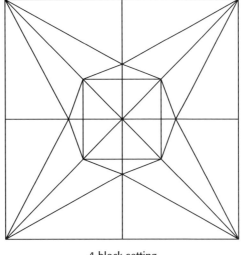

4-block setting

Left and Right

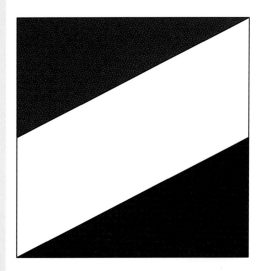

The following cutting list yields 1 block.

Fabric	Number of Pieces	Size to Cut	Location Number
White	1	3¼" x 6½"	1
Navy	1	3¼" x 6½"	2
Red	1	3¼" x 6½"	3

8 rows of 6 blocks

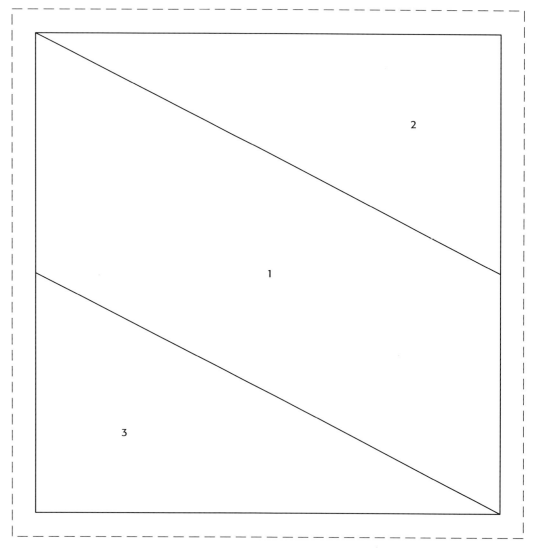

Left and Right
Foundation pattern

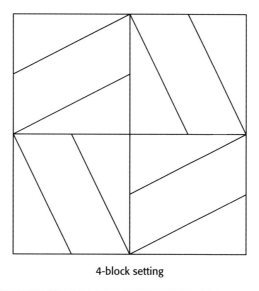

4-block setting

Lobster Claw

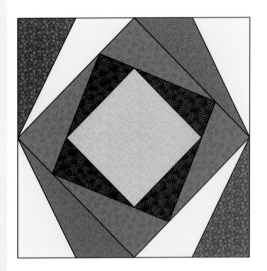

The following cutting list yields 1 block.

Fabric	Number of Pieces	Size to Cut	Location Number
Gold	1 ▢	3" x 3"	1
Black	4 ▭	1½" x 3"	2, 3, 4, 5
Medium moss green	4 ▭	2" x 3½"	6, 7, 8, 9
Rust	2 ▭	2" x 4¼"	10, 12
Cream	2 ▭	2" x 4¼"	11, 13
	2 ▭	2" x 3½"	15, 17
Dark moss green	2 ▭	2" x 3½"	14, 16

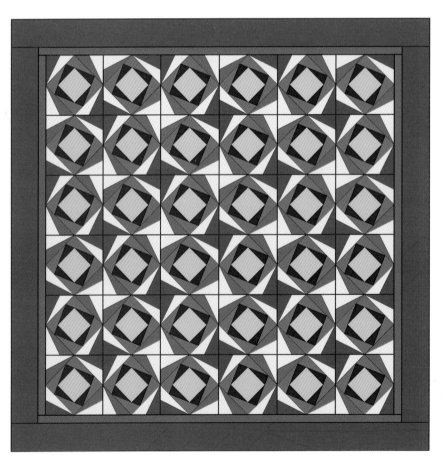

6 rows of 6 blocks

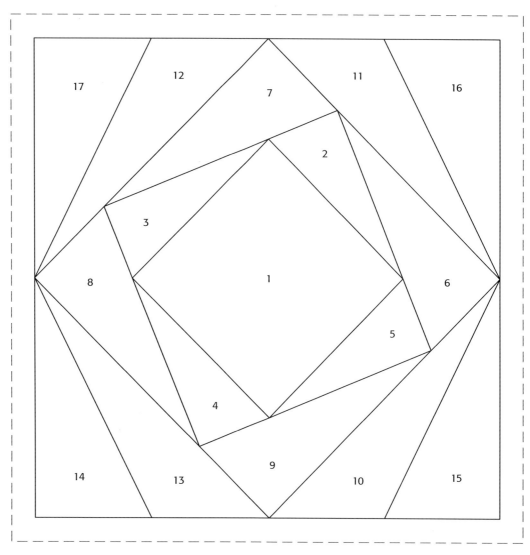

Lobster Claw
Foundation pattern

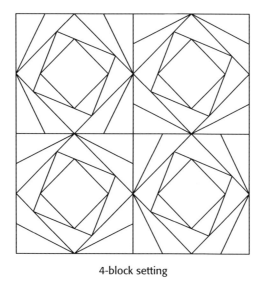

4-block setting

Magic Box

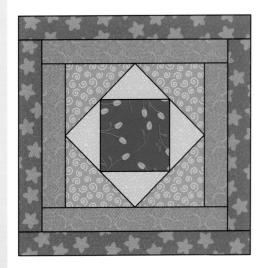

The following cutting list yields 1 block.

Fabric	Number of Pieces	Size to Cut	Location Number
Royal blue	1 ☐	2¼" x 2¼"	1
Light blue	2 ◰	2¼" x 2¼"	2, 3, 4, 5
Gold	2 ◰	2¾" x 2¾"	6, 7, 8, 9
Medium blue	2 ▭	1¼" x 3¾"	10, 11
	2 ▭	1¼" x 4¾"	12, 13
Orange	2 ▭	1¼" x 4¾"	14, 15
	2 ▭	1¼" x 5¾"	16, 17

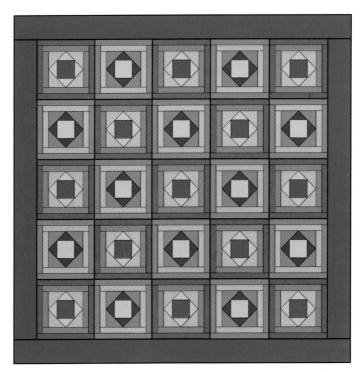

5 rows of 5 blocks

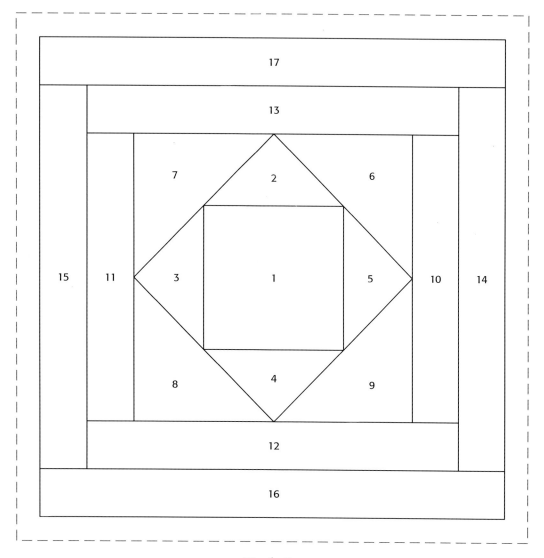

Magic Box
Foundation pattern

FOR A DIFFERENT LOOK

Try switching the location of the colors in these blocks as shown in the quilt on the facing page.

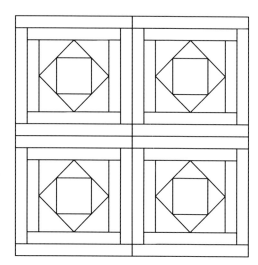

4-block setting

Market Square

The following cutting list yields 2 blocks.

Fabric	Number of Pieces	Size to Cut	Location Number
Navy	1 ◻	2¾" x 2¾"	A1
	2 ▭	2" x 4¼"	A3
	2 ▭	2¼" x 5¾"	B1
	2 ▭	1¾" x 3"	B3
Yellow	2 ▭	1¾" x 3"	A2
Gold	2 ▭	2¼" x 5¾"	A4
Red	2 ▭	2" x 4¼"	B2
	1 ◻	2¾" x 2¾"	B4

6 rows of 6 blocks

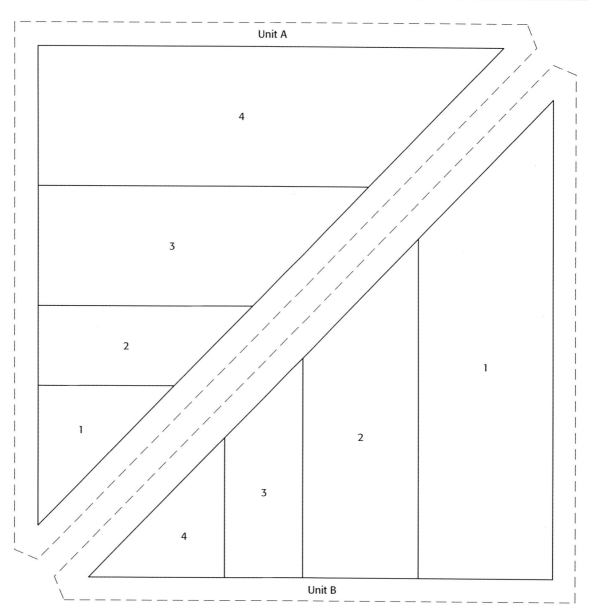

Unit A

Unit B

Market Square
Foundation patterns

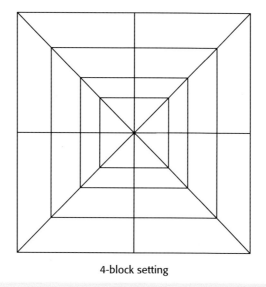

4-block setting

Milkmaid's Star

The following cutting list yields 2 blocks.

Fabric	Number of Pieces	Size to Cut	Location Number
White	4 ▭	3¼" x 4½"	1, 3
Dark purple	2 ▢	4¼" x 4¼"	2
Raspberry	1 ◹	3¾" x 3¾"	4
Purple	1 ◹	3¾" x 3¾"	5

6 rows of 6 blocks

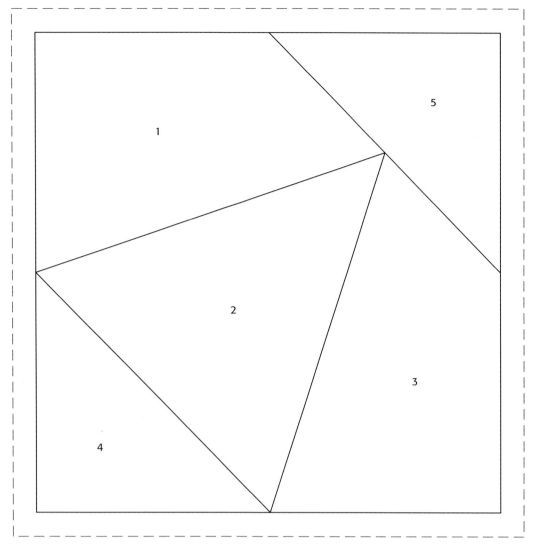

Milkmaid's Star
Foundation pattern

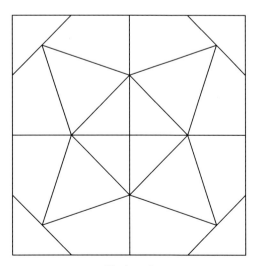

4-block setting

Missouri Windmills

The following cutting list yields 1 block.

Fabric	Number of Pieces	Size to Cut	Location Number
Orange	1	4½" x 5¾"	A1
Black	2	2½" x 5¾"	A2, B2
Yellow	1	4½" x 5¾"	B1

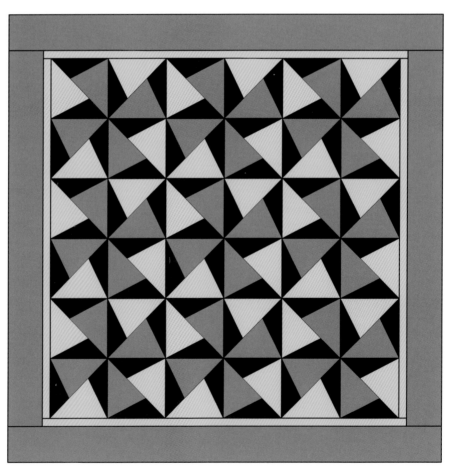

6 rows of 6 blocks

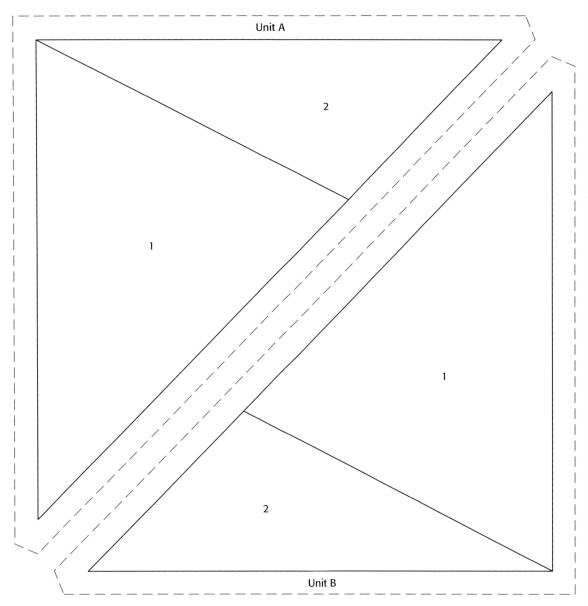

Unit A

2

1

1

2

Unit B

Missouri Windmills
Foundation patterns

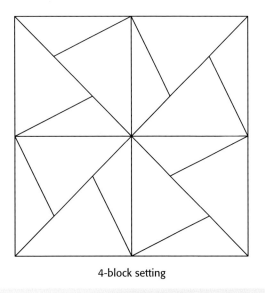

4-block setting

Morning Star

The following cutting list yields 2 blocks.

Fabric	Number of Pieces	Size to Cut	Location Number
Gold	1	2¾" x 2¾"	A1
Blue stars	2	2½" x 4"	A2
	2	2" x 4½"	B5
White	4	3¼" x 4½"	A3, B4
	2	2" x 3¼"	B6
Navy	2	2" x 4¼"	A4
	2	3" x 5"	B3
Yellow	2	1½" x 2¾"	A5
	2	1¾" x 2¾"	B2
Royal blue	1	3" x 3"	A6
	1	2¾" x 2¾"	B1

6 rows of 6 blocks

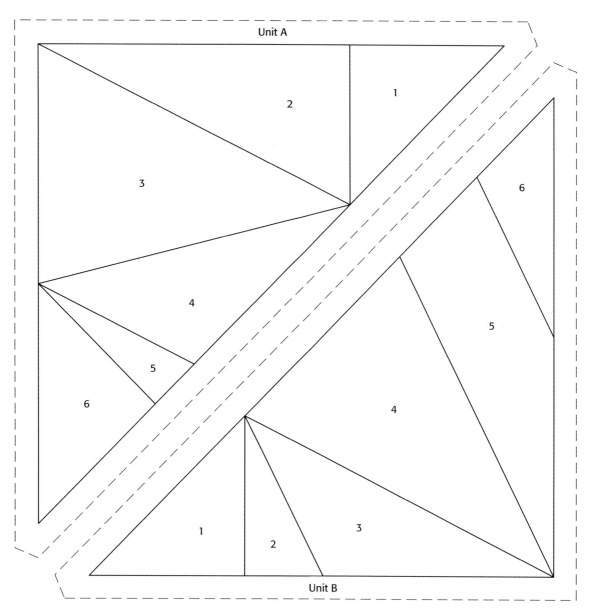

Unit A

2

1

3

6

4

5

5

6

4

1

2

3

Unit B

Morning Star
Foundation patterns

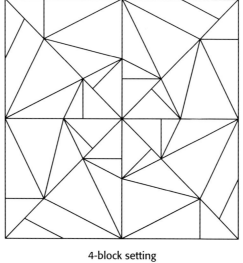

4-block setting

Mosaic Square

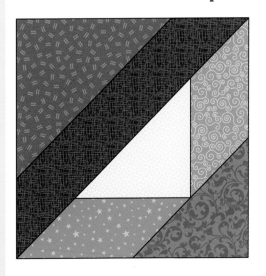

The following cutting list yields 2 blocks.

Fabric	Number of Pieces	Size to Cut	Location Number
Cream	1	3¾" x 3¾"	1
Orange	2	2" x 4½"	2
Gold	2	2" x 4½"	3
Rust	1	3¾" x 3¾"	4
Dark brown	2	2" x 7¾"	5
Medium brown	1	4½" x 4½"	6

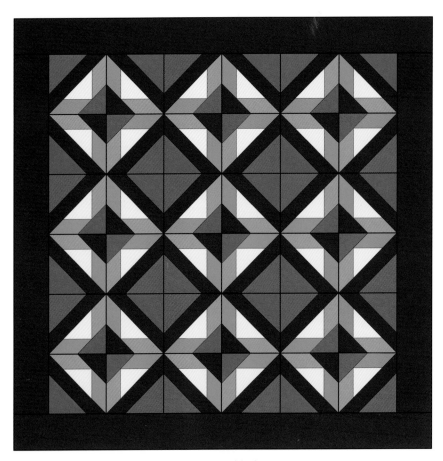

6 rows of 6 blocks

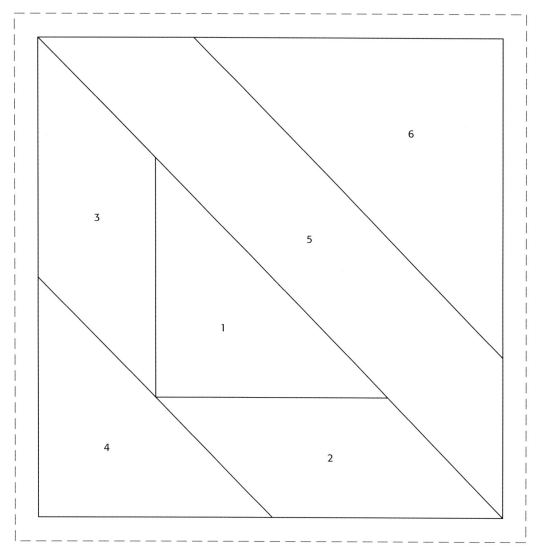

Mosaic Square
Foundation pattern

4-block setting

Mosaic Tiles

The following cutting list yields 1 block.

Fabric	Number of Pieces	Size to Cut	Location Number
Cream	1 □	2" x 2"	1
Gold	1 □	2" x 2"	2
Tan	1 ▭	3¼" x 3¾"	3
Dark brown	1 ▭	3¼" x 5"	4
Red	1 ▭	1¾" x 5¾"	5

8 rows of 6 blocks

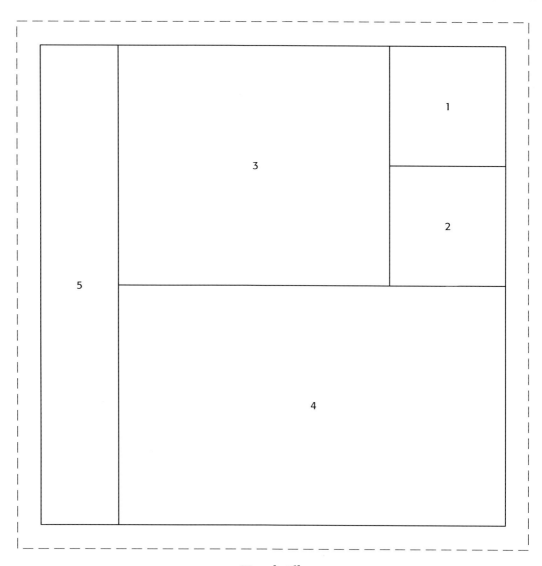

Mosaic Tiles
Foundation pattern

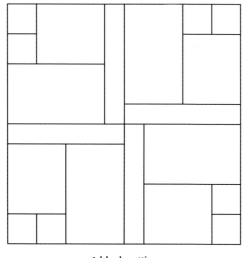

4-block setting

Mosaic Triangles

The following cutting list yields 2 blocks.

Fabric	Number of Pieces	Size to Cut	Location Number
Royal blue	1 ◻	3¾" x 3¾"	1
Dark red	1 ◻	3¾" x 3¾"	2
Cream	2 ◻	3¾" x 3¾"	3, 4
Red	2 ▭	2½" x 7¾"	5
Navy	1 ◻	3¾" x 3¾"	6

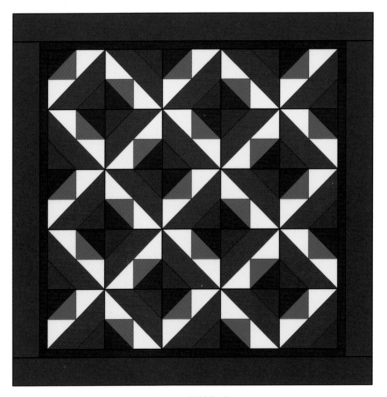

5 rows of 5 blocks

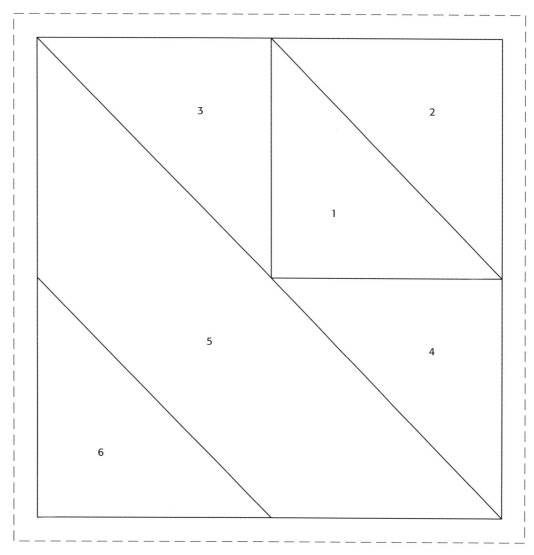

Mosaic Triangles
Foundation pattern

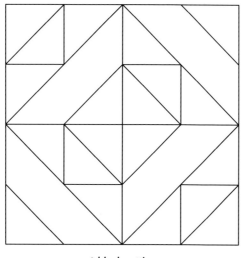

4-block setting

New Jersey

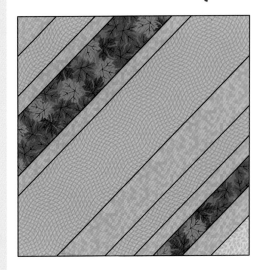

The following cutting list yields 2 blocks.

Fabric	Number of Pieces		Size to Cut	Location Number
Gold	1	◻	2" x 2"	1
	2	▭	1" x 3¾"	3
	2	▭	1" x 6¼"	5
	2	▭	1½" x 6¾"	7
	2	▭	1" x 4¼"	9
	2	▭	1¼" x 3"	11
Medium blue	2	▭	1½" x 2¼"	2
	2	▭	2¼" x 7¾"	6
	2	▭	1¼" x 5¼"	8
Royal blue	2	▭	1¾" x 5½"	4
	2	▭	1¼" x 3¾"	10
Light blue	1	◻	2" x 2"	12

8 rows of 6 blocks

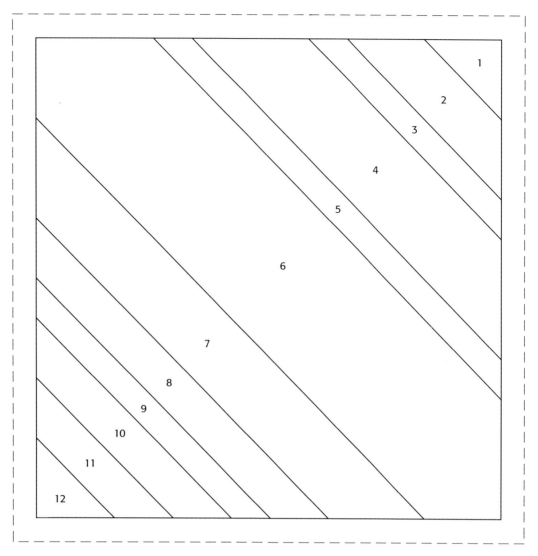

New Jersey
Foundation pattern

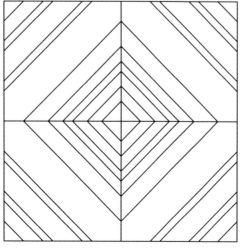

4-block setting

New Star

The following cutting list yields 2 blocks.

Fabric	Number of Pieces	Size to Cut	Location Number
Royal blue	2 ☐	5¾" x 5¾"	1
Yellow	2 ▭	2" x 4½"	2
Red	2 ▭	2" x 6¼"	3
Light blue	1 ◺	3¾" x 3¾"	4

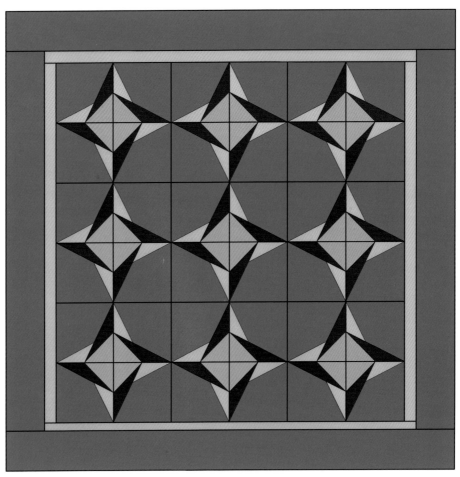

6 rows of 6 blocks

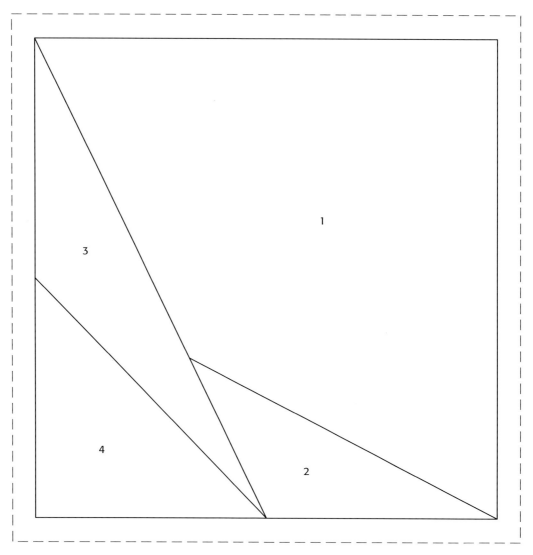

New Star
Foundation pattern

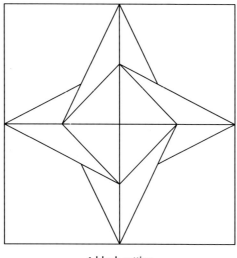

4-block setting

Next-Door Neighbor

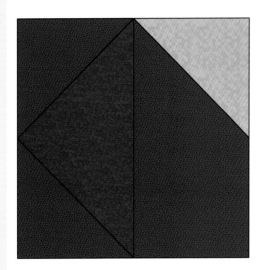

The following cutting list yields 4 blocks.

Fabric	Number of Pieces	Size to Cut	Location Number
Red	1 ⊠	6½" x 6½"	1
Navy	4 ◺	3¾" x 3¾"	2, 3
	4 ▭	3¼" x 5¾"	4
Gold	2 ◺	3¾" x 3¾"	5

8 rows of 6 blocks

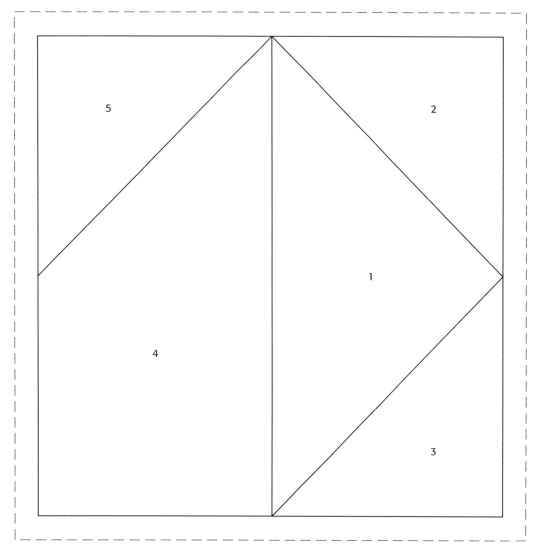

Next-Door Neighbor
Foundation pattern

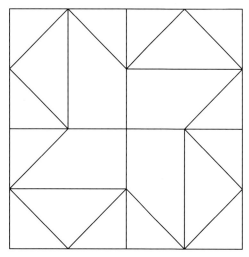

4-block setting

The Palm

The following cutting list yields 1 block.

Fabric	Number of Pieces	Size to Cut	Location Number
Light blue	2 ▭	2" x 6"	A1, B7
	2 ▭	2" x 4¾"	A3, B5
	2 ▭	2" x 3½"	A5, B3
	1 ◺	2½" x 2½"	A7, B1
Dark blue and red print	2 ▭	1¾" x 6"	A2, B6
	2 ▭	1½" x 4¾"	A4, B4
	2 ▭	1½" x 2½"	A6, B2

6 rows of 6 blocks

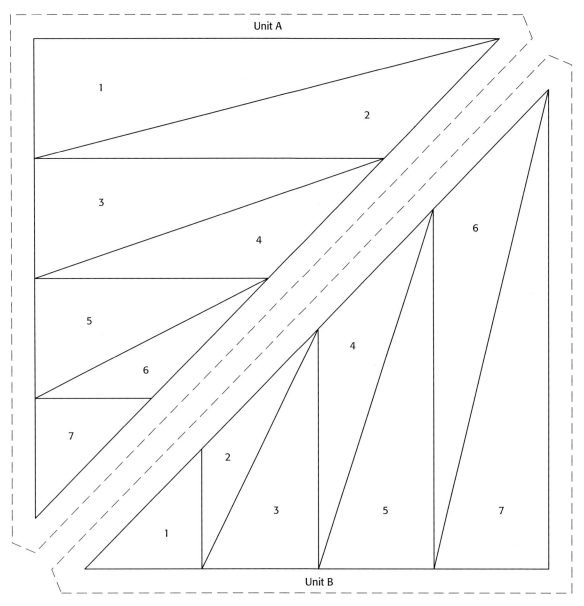

Unit A

1

2

3

4

5

6

6

7

4

2

1

3

5

7

Unit B

The Palm
Foundation patterns

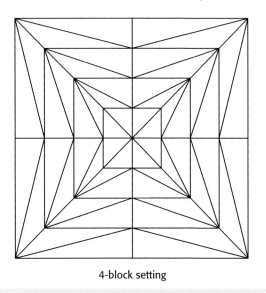

4-block setting

Peace and Plenty

The following cutting list yields 4 blocks.

Fabric	Number of Pieces	Size to Cut	Location Number
Tan	4 ◻	3¾" x 3¾"	A1, B2
	1 ⊠	6½" x 6½"	A3
Brown	2 ◻	3¾" x 3¾"	A2
Chocolate brown	2 ◻	3¾" x 3¾"	B1
Rust	1 ⊠	6½" x 6½"	B3

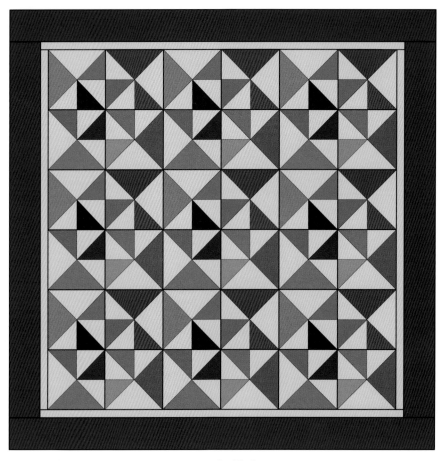

6 rows of 6 blocks

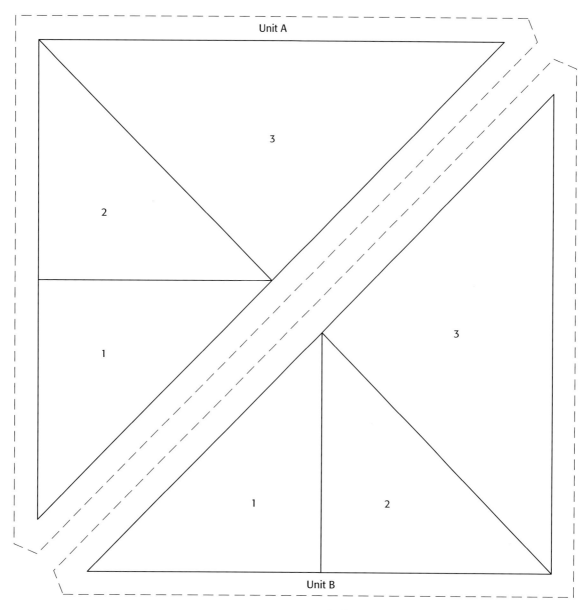

Unit A

3

2

1

3

1

2

Unit B

Peace and Plenty
Foundation patterns

FOR A DIFFERENT LOOK

*Try making these blocks
in a variety of scrappy
combinations as shown
in the quilt on the facing
page.*

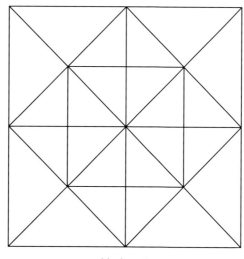

4-block setting

Perpetual Motion

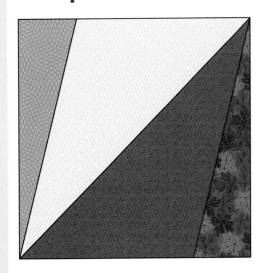

The following cutting list yields 1 block.

Fabric	Number of Pieces	Size to Cut	Location Number
Cream	1	4½" x 7¾"	1
Rust	1	4½" x 7¾"	2
Royal blue	1	2" x 6"	3
Medium blue	1	2" x 6"	4

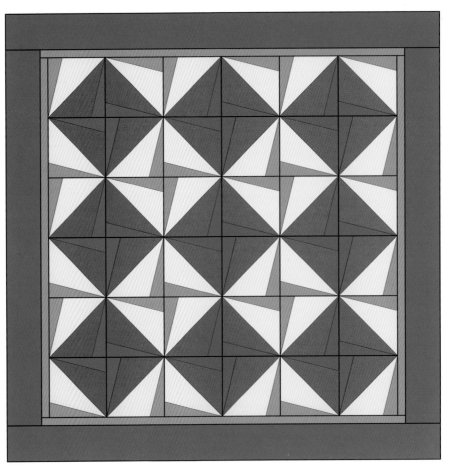

6 rows of 6 blocks

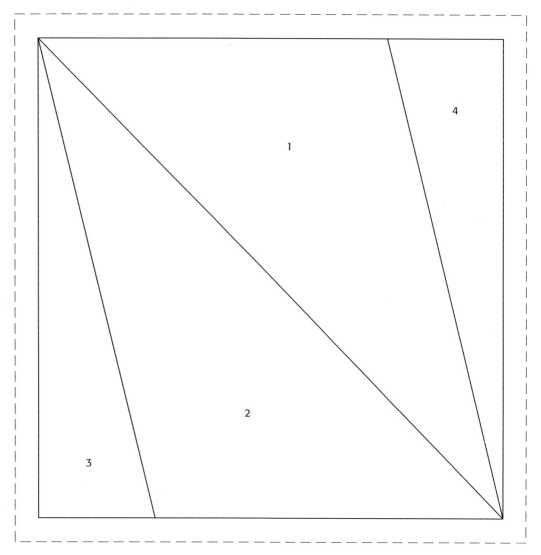

Perpetual Motion
Foundation pattern

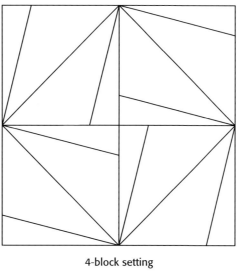

4-block setting

Peter's Quilt

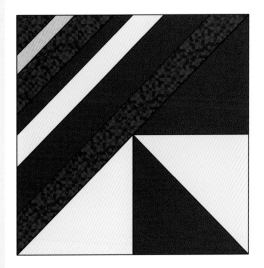

The following cutting list yields 2 blocks.

Fabric	Number of Pieces	Size to Cut	Location Number
Red	2 ◻	3¾" x 3¾"	1, 3
	2 ▭	1½" x 6¾"	6
	2 ▭	1" x 4¼"	8
Cream	2 ◻	3¾" x 3¾"	2, 4
	2 ▭	1¼" x 5¼"	7
Navy	2 ▭	1½" x 8"	5
	2 ▭	1½" x 3¾"	9
	1 ◻	2" x 2"	11
Gold	2 ▭	1" x 2½"	10

6 rows of 6 blocks

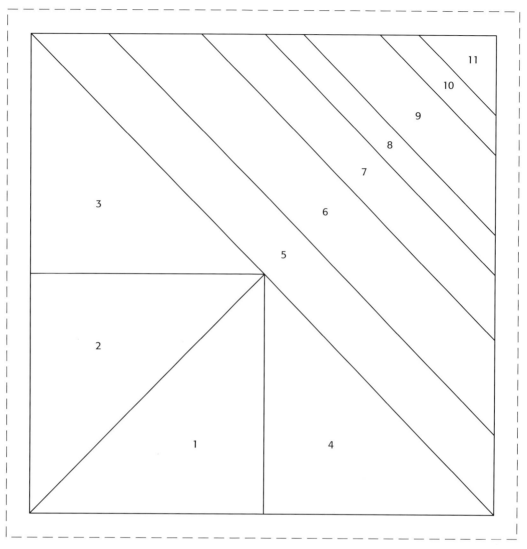

Peter's Quilt
Foundation pattern

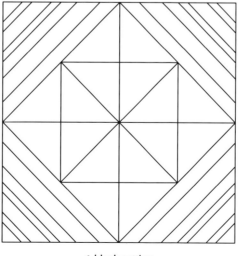

4-block setting

Pinwheel

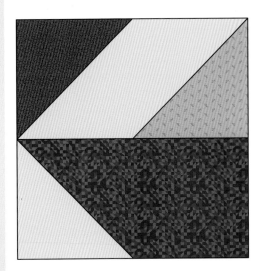

The following cutting list yields 2 blocks.

Fabric	Number of Pieces		Size to Cut	Location Number
Cream	2	▭	3¼" x 4¼"	1
	1	◹	3¾" x 3¾"	5
Gold	1	◹	3¾" x 3¾"	2
Purple	1	◹	3¾" x 3¾"	3
Dark green	2	▭	3¼" x 5¾"	4

8 rows of 6 blocks

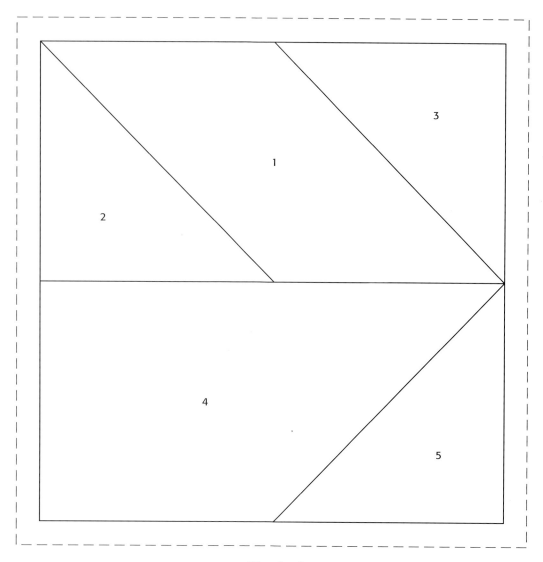

Pinwheel
Foundation pattern

FOR A DIFFERENT LOOK

Try making these blocks in four slightly different color combinations as shown in the quilt on the facing page.

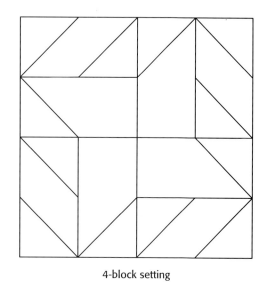

4-block setting

Pinwheel Parade

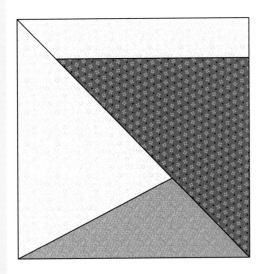

The following cutting list yields 2 blocks.

Fabric	Number of Pieces	Size to Cut	Location Number
Red geometric	1 ◻	5¼" x 5¼"	A1
Cream	2 ▭	1¾" x 5¾"	A2
	2 ▭	4" x 5¾"	B1
Gold	2 ▭	2½" x 5¾"	B2

8 rows of 6 blocks

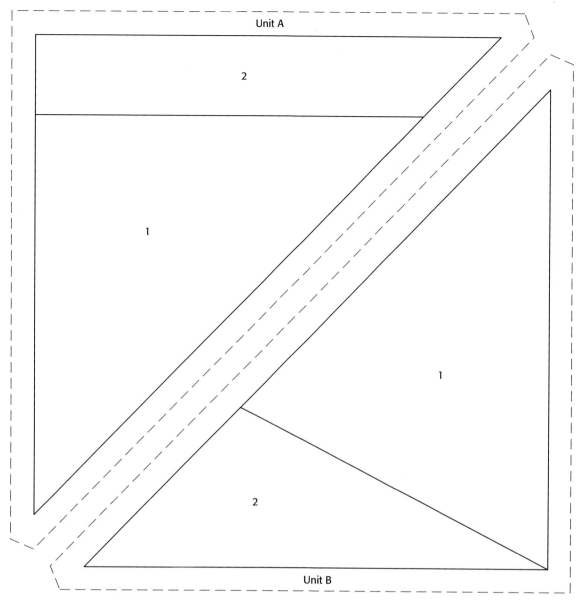

Unit A

2

1

1

2

Unit B

Pinwheel Parade
Foundation patterns

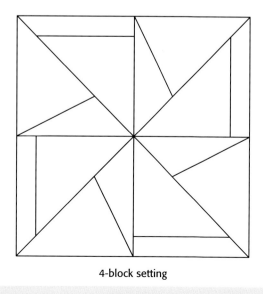

4-block setting

Pinwheel Star

The following cutting list yields 2 blocks.

Fabric	Number of Pieces	Size to Cut	Location Number
Navy	2	2½" x 7¾"	1
Medium blue	2	2" x 7¾"	2
Light yellow	2	2" x 6½"	3
Orange	2	2" x 4½"	4
Yellow	2	2" x 6½"	5
Cream	1	3¾" x 3¾"	6
Light blue	1	3¾" x 3¾"	7

6 rows of 6 blocks

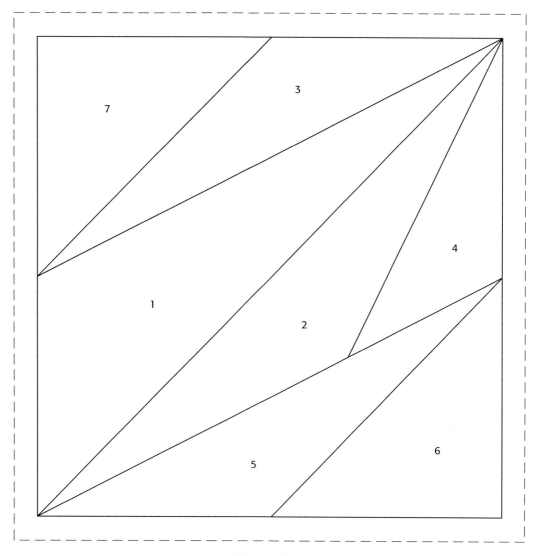

Pinwheel Star
Foundation pattern

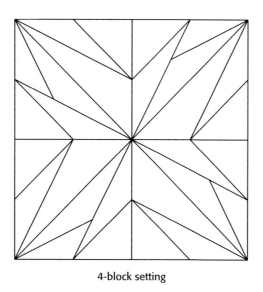

4-block setting

Plain Sailing

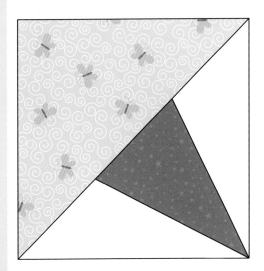

The following cutting list yields 2 blocks.

Fabric	Number of Pieces	Size to Cut	Location Number
Orange	2 ▭	3¼" x 4½"	1
White	4 ▭	2½" x 5¾"	2, 3
Light green	1 ◹	6¼" x 6¼"	4

6 rows of 6 blocks

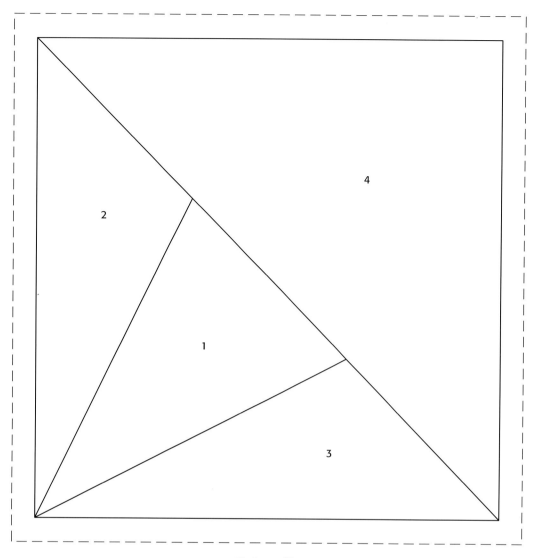

Plain Sailing
Foundation pattern

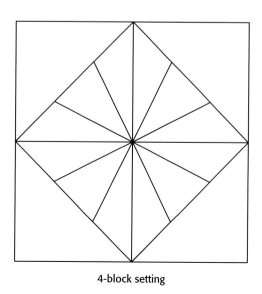

4-block setting

Riviera

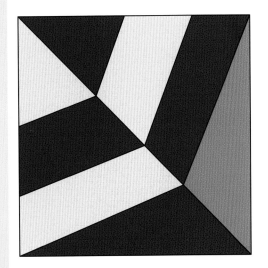

The following cutting list yields 1 block.

Fabric	Number of Pieces	Size to Cut	Location Number
Navy	1	2½" x 3¼"	A1
	1	2" x 4½"	A3
	1	2¾" x 5¾"	B1
	1	2¼" x 3¾"	B3
Light yellow	1	2¼" x 3¾"	A2
	1	2" x 4½"	B2
	1	2½" x 3¼"	B4
Reddish orange	1	2¾" x 5¾"	A4

8 rows of 6 blocks

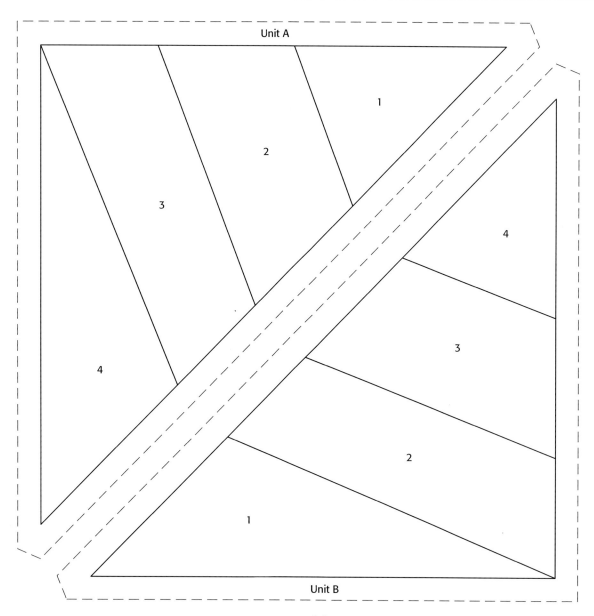

Unit A

1

2

3

4

4

3

2

1

Unit B

Riviera
Foundation patterns

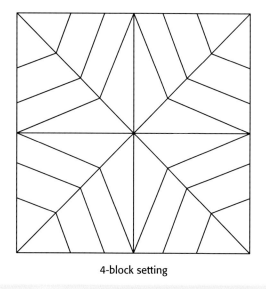

4-block setting

Road to Fortune

The following cutting list yields 2 blocks.

Fabric	Number of Pieces	Size to Cut	Location Number
White	4	2¼" x 4½"	A1, B4
	4	3¼" x 4¾"	A3, B2
Dark turquoise	4	1½" x 4¾"	A2, B3
Aqua	2	3¼" x 3¾"	A4
Purple	1	3¾" x 3¾"	B1

6 rows of 6 blocks

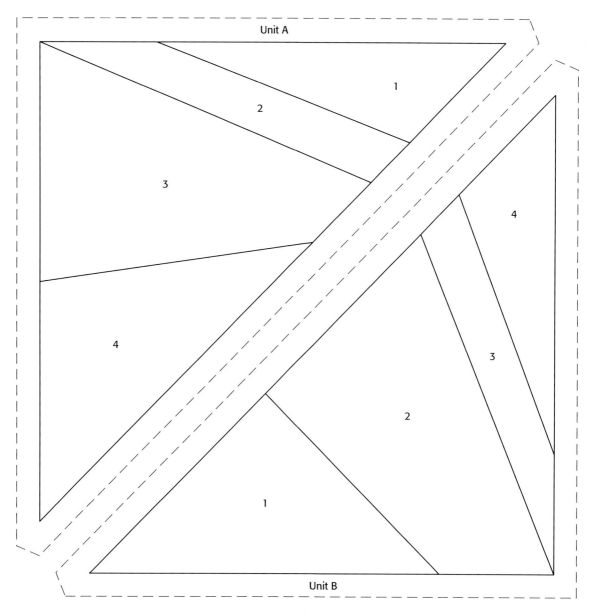

Unit A

1

2

3

4

4

3

2

1

Unit B

Road to Fortune
Foundation patterns

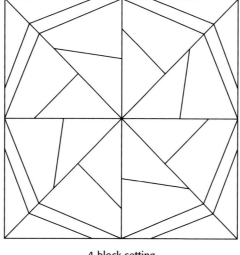

4-block setting

Spider Web

The following cutting list yields 1 block.

Fabric	Number of Pieces	Size to Cut	Location Number
Light blue	1	2¼" x 4½"	A1
Red	1	2¼" x 3¼"	A2
	2	2" x 5"	A4, B5
	1	2" x 2½"	A6
Navy	2	2" x 2½"	A3, B6
	1	2" x 5"	A5
White	1	2¼" x 4½"	B1
	1	2" x 2½"	B3
Medium blue	1	2¼" x 3¼"	B2
	1	2" x 5"	B4

8 rows of 6 blocks

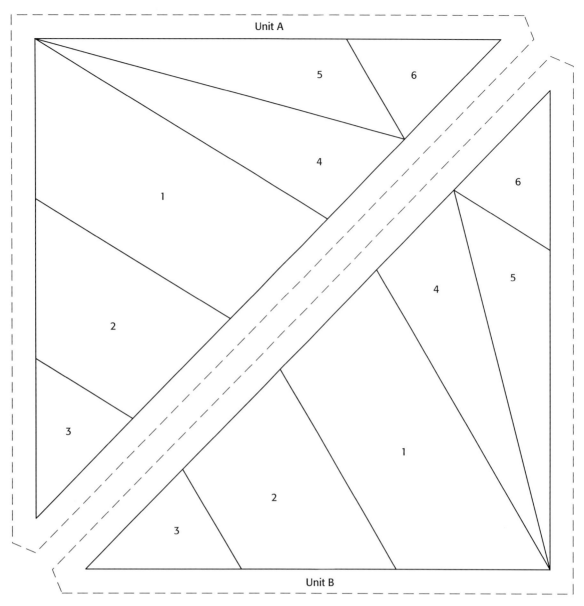

Unit A

5   6

4

1

6

2

5

3

4

1

2

3

Unit B

Spider Web
Foundation patterns

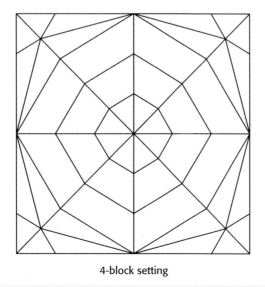

4-block setting

Spinning Color Wheel

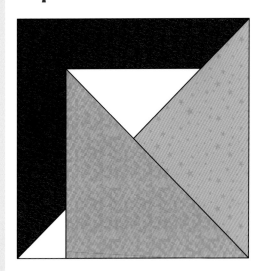

The following cutting list yields 4 blocks.

Fabric	Number of Pieces	Size to Cut	Location Number
White	1 ⊠	4½" x 4½"	A1
	2 ◳	2¼" x 2¼"	B2
Black	8 ▭	1¾" x 5¾"	A2, B1
Gold	1 ⊠	6½" x 6½"	A3
Orange	2 ◳	5¼" x 5¼"	B3

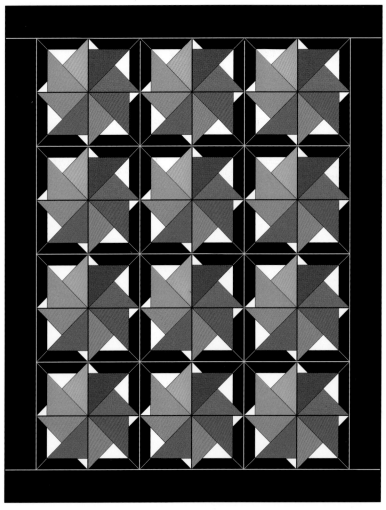

8 rows of 6 blocks

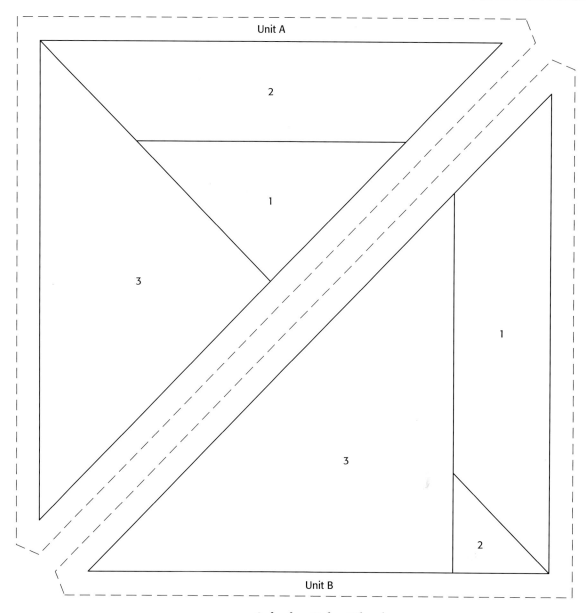

Unit A

2

1

3

1

3

2

Unit B

Spinning Color Wheel
Foundation patterns

For a Different Look

*Try making these blocks
in four different colors as
shown in the quilt on the
facing page.*

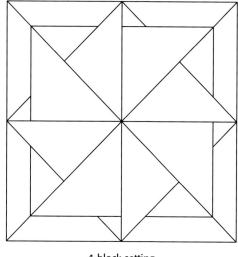

4-block setting

Split Star

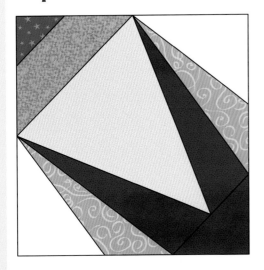

The following cutting list yields 2 blocks.

Fabric	Number of Pieces	Size to Cut	Location Number
Yellow	2 ▭	4¼" x 5"	1
Navy	4 ▭	2" x 5¼"	2, 3
	1 ◇	2¾" x 2¾"	10
Medium blue	4 ▭	1¾" x 5"	4, 5
Light blue	4 ▭	2¾" x 3¼"	6, 7
Gold	2 ▭	1¾" x 4¼"	8
Dark blue	1 ◇	2¼" x 2¼"	9

6 rows of 6 blocks

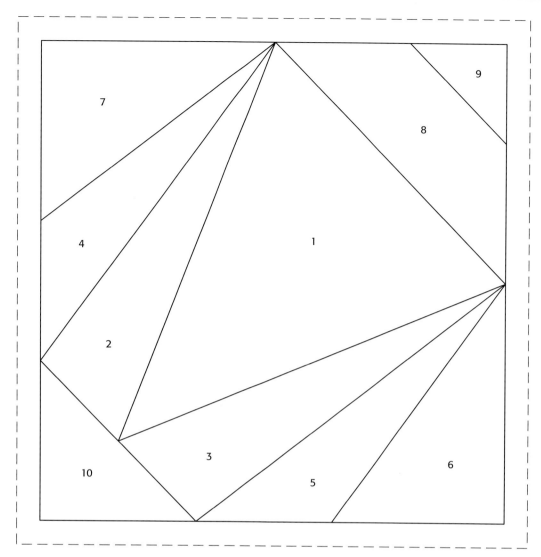

Split Star
Foundation pattern

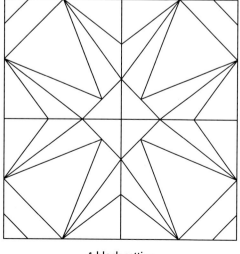

4-block setting

Star Cross

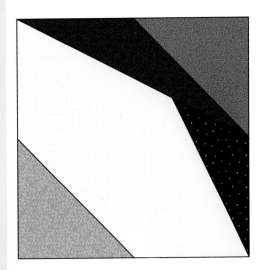

The following cutting list yields 2 blocks.

Fabric	Number of Pieces	Size to Cut	Location Number
Cream	2 ▭	3¾" x 7¾"	1
Yellow	1 ◻	3¾" x 3¾"	2
Black	2 ▭	2" x 4½"	3
Red	2 ▭	2" x 6½"	4
Green	1 ◻	3¾" x 3¾"	5

6 rows of 6 blocks

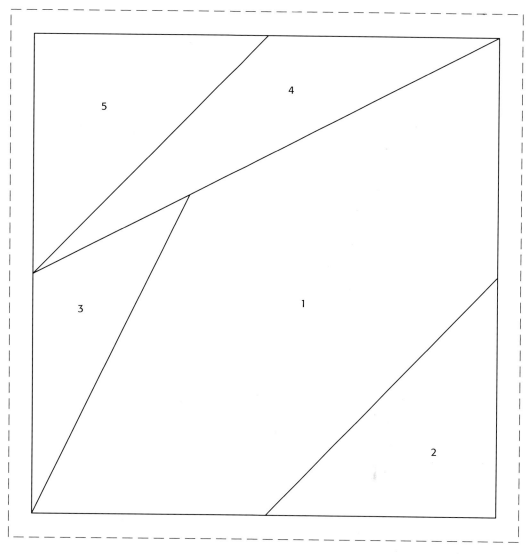

Star Cross
Foundation pattern

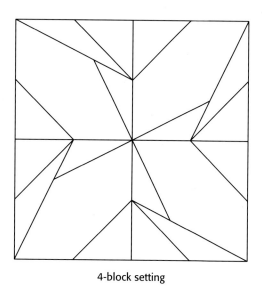

4-block setting

Storm Signal

The following cutting list yields 2 blocks.

Fabric	Number of Pieces	Size to Cut	Location Number
White	2 ☐	3¼" x 3¼"	1
Medium purple	1 ⊠	5" x 5"	2, 3
Peach	1 ◺	2¾" x 2¾"	4
Green	1 ◺	6¼" x 6¼"	5

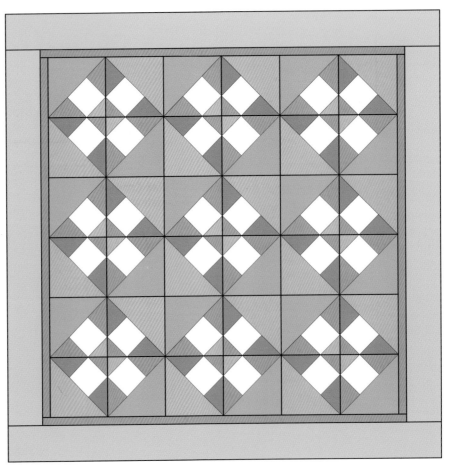

6 rows of 6 blocks

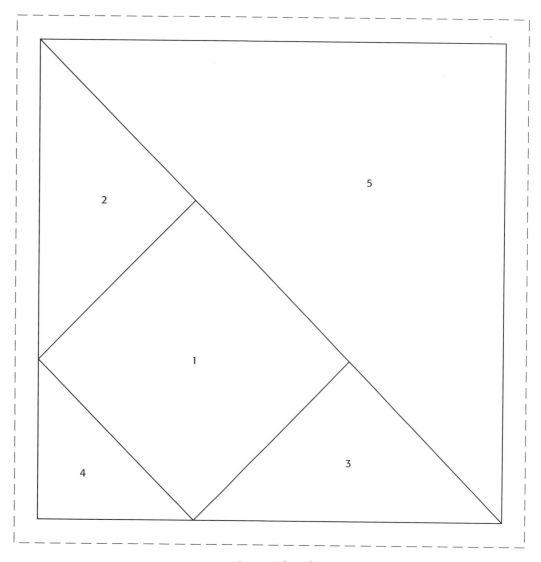

Storm Signal
Foundation pattern

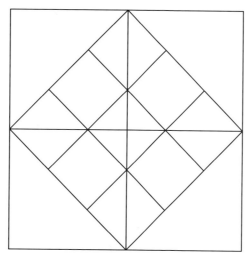

4-block setting

Sugar Cone

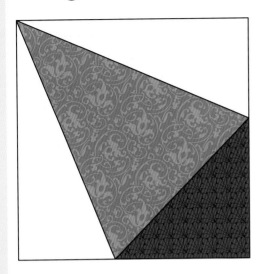

The following cutting list yields 2 blocks.

Fabric	Number of Pieces	Size to Cut	Location Number
Blue	2	5" x 6"	1
Light blue	4	3" x 5¾"	2, 3
Red	1	4" x 4"	4

8 rows of 6 blocks

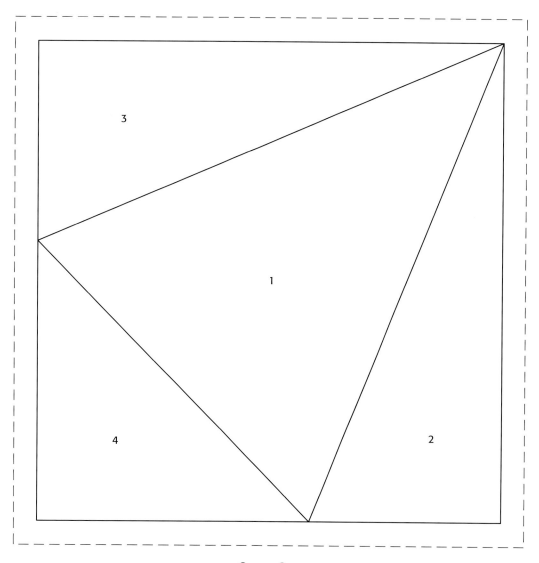

Sugar Cone
Foundation pattern

FOR A DIFFERENT LOOK

Try switching the location of the colors in these blocks as shown in the quilt on the facing page.

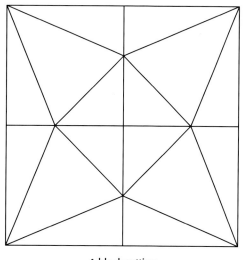

4-block setting

Susannah

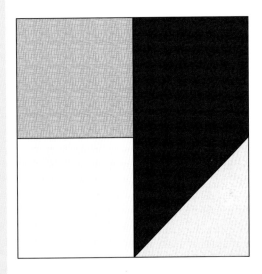

The following cutting list yields 2 blocks.

Fabric	Number of Pieces	Size to Cut	Location Number
Tan	2 ☐	3¼" x 3¼"	1
Cream	2 ☐	3¼" x 3¼"	2
	1 ◻	3¾" x 3¾"	4
Red	2 ▭	3¼" x 5¾"	3

8 rows of 6 blocks

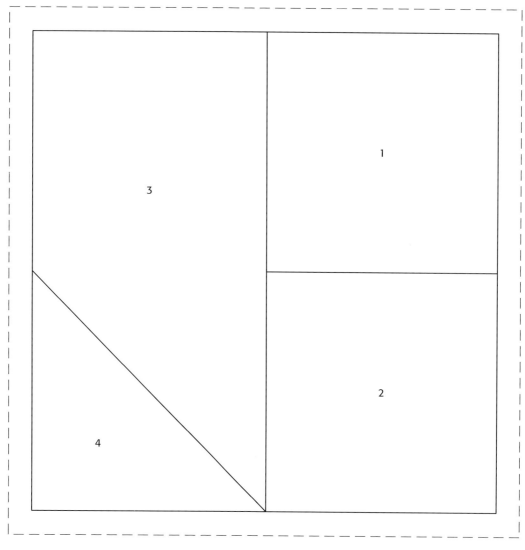

Susannah
Foundation pattern

FOR A DIFFERENT LOOK

Try making these blocks in two slightly different color combinations as shown in the quilt on the facing page.

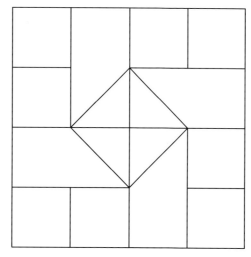

4-block setting

Target

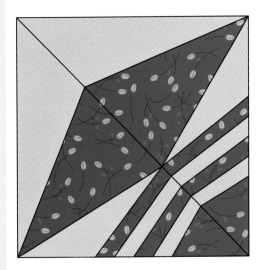

The following cutting list yields 1 block.

Fabric	Number of Pieces	Size to Cut	Location Number
Yellow	2 ▭	2½" x 5¾"	A1, B8
	2 ▭	1¾" x 4½"	A3, B6
	2 ▭	1¼" x 3"	A5, B4
	2 ▭	1¼" x 2¼"	A7, B2
Blue	2 ▭	3¼" x 4½"	A2, B7
	2 ▭	1¼" x 3¼"	A4, B5
	2 ▭	1¼" x 2½"	A6, B3
	2 ▭	2" x 2½"	A8, B1

6 rows of 6 blocks

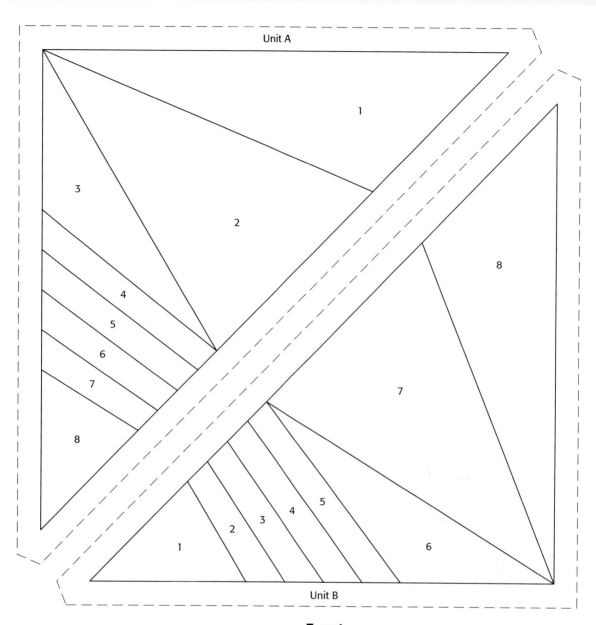

Unit A

1

3

2

8

4

5

6

7

7

8

8

1

2

3

4

5

6

Unit B

Target
Foundation patterns

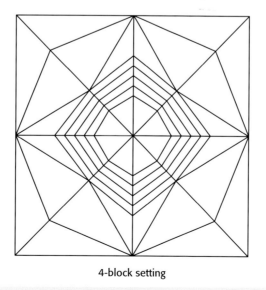

4-block setting

Turkey Giblets

The following cutting list yields 1 block.

Fabric	Number of Pieces	Size to Cut	Location Number
Cream	1 ▢	4¼" x 4¼"	A1
	2 ▭	2¾" x 3¼"	B2, B3
Red	1 ▢	4¼" x 4¼"	B1
	2 ▭	2¾" x 3¼"	A2, A3

6 rows of 6 blocks

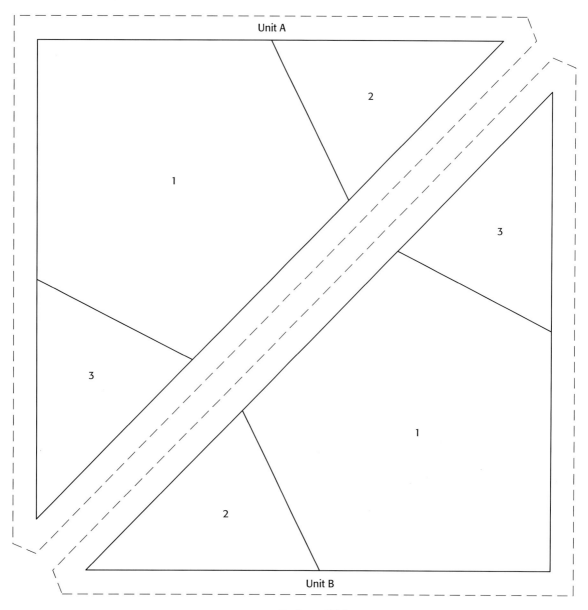

Unit A

2

1

3

3

1

2

Unit B

Turkey Giblets
Foundation patterns

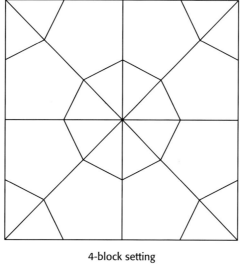

4-block setting

Wheels

The following cutting list yields 4 blocks.

Fabric	Number of Pieces	Size to Cut	Location Number
Cream	1 ⊠	6½" x 6½"	1
Red	1 ⊠	6½" x 6½"	2
Black floral	4 ▭	2½" x 7¾"	3
Gold	2 ◻	3¾" x 3¾"	4

8 rows of 6 blocks

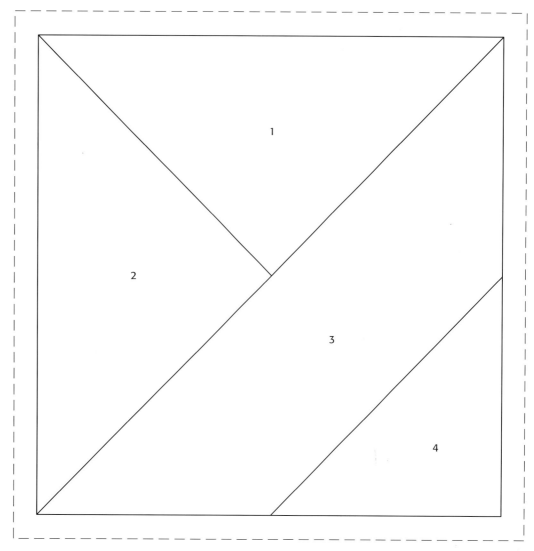

Wheels
Foundation pattern

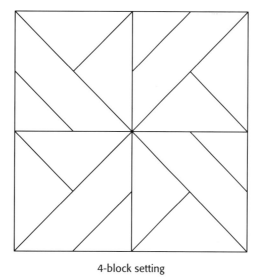

4-block setting

Windmill

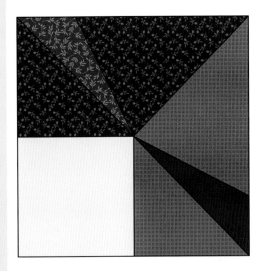

The following cutting list yields 2 blocks.

Fabric	Number of Pieces	Size to Cut	Location Number
Black	2 ▭	3½" x 4½"	A1
	1 ◻	3¾" x 3¾"	B3
Steel blue	2 ▭	3½" x 4½"	A2
	1 ◻	3¾" x 3¾"	B2
Navy	2 ▭	1¾" x 4¼"	A3
Red	2 ▭	1¾" x 4¼"	A4
Cream	2 ◻	3¼" x 3¼"	B1

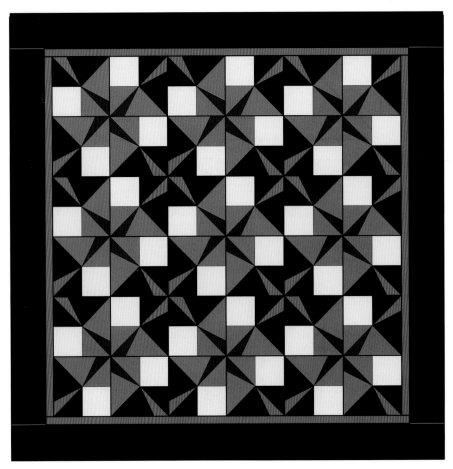

6 rows of 6 blocks

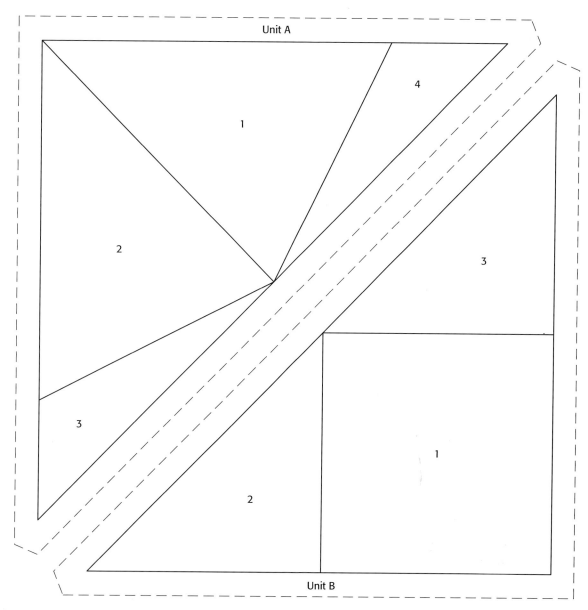

Unit A

1

4

2

3

3

2

1

Unit B

Windmill
Foundation patterns

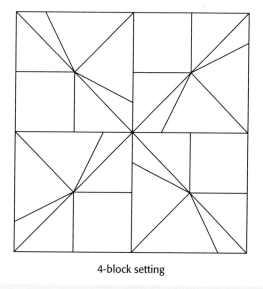

4-block setting

About the Author

Author, teacher, fabric designer, and award-winning quiltmaker Nancy Mahoney has enjoyed making quilts for more than 20 years. An impressive range of her beautiful quilts has been featured in many books and national quilt magazines.

Quilt Block Bonanza is Nancy's fifth book with Martingale & Company. Her other bestselling books include *Patchwork Showcase* (2004) and *Basket Bonanza* (2005).

Almost entirely self-taught, Nancy likes to explore new ways to use traditional blocks and updated techniques to create quilts that are easy to make.

Nancy lives in Palm Coast, Florida, with her life partner of 30 years, Tom, and their umbrella cockatoo, Prince. When Nancy's not quilting, she enjoys gardening, walking on the beach, and shopping for antiques.